"God made the desert, then in a fit of rage he threw stones onto it."

Berber saying

Blank page

Carpe Diem

... but when I said that nothing had been done I erred in one important matter. We had definitely committed ourselves and were halfway out of our ruts. We had put down our passage money— booked a sailing to Bombay. This may sound too simple, but is great in consequence. Until one is committed, there is hesitancy, the chance to draw back, always ineffectiveness. Concerning all acts of initiative (and creation), there is one elementary truth, the ignorance of which kills countless ideas and splendid plans: that the moment one definitely commits oneself, then Providence moves too. All sorts of things occur to help one that would never otherwise have occurred. A whole stream of events issues from the decision, raising in one's favour all manner of unforeseen incidents and meetings and material assistance, which no man could have dreamt would have come his way. I learned a deep respect for one of Goethe's couplets:

Whatever you can do or dream you can, begin it.
Boldness has genius, power and magic in it!

W.H.Murray *The Scottish Himalayan Expedition* (1951)

Blank page

Contents

one

A story of adventure and trauma (yours)

- Starting point - what are your race goals?
- Why are you doing this?
- Reality check - and soul searching (you'll do plenty on the way round, start now)
- Where are you starting from and how much time do you have?
- This book is for anyone thinking about running the famous marathon of the sands, Kalahari or other great races. From the novice aiming to get round, to the experienced runner having a shot at the top 100.
- I cannot emphasize preparation enough.
- Prepare your body, mind and spirit.
- Prepare your kit.
- Prepare your nipple plasters …

A unique race

So you want to run an ultra-marathon? And why not?

Have you ever wondered what it is like to run marathons, every day, in the Sahara, for a week?

There are sandy desert races all around the world to test your body mind and spirit. All in breathtaking scenery far away from the daily hamster wheel that we usually live in.

This book is about how to go from zero to hero. I'm a family practitioner and no running god. I now run ultra marathons for fun, just to see how far and how fast an ordinary runner can go. I am not an elite, but bring my medical experience to help you prepare for your first desert marathon.

The most popular desert race is the Marathon des Sables (MdS) and many examples are taken directly from this. Now well over its thirtieth year. I ran this and had an amazing time. While slanting towards the MdS in terms of detail, this is all about preparing for any multi-day, marathon and ultra-marathon distance race in a hot sandy desert. I do know there are other types of desert, but this is largely about the hot sandy type.

* * *

Desert racing is famous around the world for being tough. The heat, the sand and the challenge calls to people from all around the world. It promotes self-sufficiency which is part of the unique experience. The MdS across the sands of the Sahara has run for thirty years. There haven't been many deaths so far. Each year it grows and brings runners from all walks of life and from all corners of the planet. Everyone comes for different reasons. Many push themselves right to their physical and mental limits. Doing so, they discover in beautiful unspoilt surroundings that pushing on these boundaries, they are capable of far more than they ever previously imagined.

There is more information available today in books and on the internet than has ever been accessible before. This is a two edged sword. While I believe the race rewards those who are better informed and prepared, some people feel that the really fine detail which you can uncover beforehand detracts a little from the mystery of the event. I chose to research widely before the event. For me, the defining and then trying to push through my limitations was the most enjoyable part of the challenge. Pushing yourself to your limits can be an immensely rewarding thing to do. Chasing the boundaries and pursuing what you are capable of, seems to be a common theme which emerges in conversations with nearly everyone that I've met while running ultras or adventure racing.

Some people go along to this famous race and deliberately choose not to find out too much about it in advance. I didn't subscribe to the mindset of an *unknown adventure*. I felt that it was quite a magnificent adventure all on its own. This was an event for me, bigger and more ballsy than anything I had tried before. It was further than I'd ever raced, for more days than I'd ever run, in hostile conditions I'd never met, wearing a pack which I'd never raced with. All of this was against some of the world's best runners.

Those very reasons are why I chose to attempt the Marathon des Sables (MdS). These may feel familiar and resonate. I felt that I would enjoy the race more and be able to perform to my best if I was as prepared as I could be. Being prepared as well as I could be meant finding out as much information in advance as I could. And turning up at the start line with a perfect Olympian body. With that in mind I tried (and largely failed) to prepare myself physically to be in the best shape that I could reasonably manage, while also trying to keep my job, sanity and my marriage intact. This is the book that I wish I'd held in my excited little hands, all those many long months ago.

Like a ferret on an important mission I tried to find out everything I possibly could before I went. By the time came to catch the flight to Africa, I thought that I had prepared meticulously. For the six preceding months I thought of and talked about little else. My poor family. My poor friends. My poor work colleagues and my poor patients. I thought about little else for six months, almost to the point of obsession. I learned a lot along the way. I learned a lot about the race, about preparation and about myself. I certainly came to understand quite a lot about my poor social skills. And then I discovered a whole lot more about those same things when I was out there.

If you like to be well informed, I really hope that this book will help you.

This book I could have put to good use two years before the race. I appreciate you may be reading this with less time on the clock. I will share enough throughout these pages to try and make this jolly useful at whichever point you pick it up.

Any misquotes, errors, omissions and mistakes in recollection are mine. Please send any feedback to the email address at the end. I've endeavoured to source my information from far and wide and although I have read extensively, there will be things I've missed. I can back up with hard science what I say - though I appreciate this will only be from a single rather over-opinionated point of view. With my medical background and experiences, my opinions and tips do carry some authority - but I urge you also to read widely and get your information from as many reputable sources as you can lay your paws on. And maybe one or two disreputable ones.

Will it be tough? Errr

Yup. It'll be hard. It will be hot. You will hurt at points. You will question your sanity. You will experience some very beautiful landscape and some stunning views will be shared with a thousand others. It will be hard but very memorable and an unforgettable experience. You will push the boundaries of what you can do and will come out of the other side bigger and better than before.

I read somewhere that during the race you may find it useful to have some things to think about in the tough times to help pull you through. Your family, your loved ones, your favourite pet. And if you get really hungry, of maybe eating your favourite pet.

There is a lot of sand. There are a lot of hills. It's quite hot and you carry a lot of stuff. At no point during the MdS or any of the other smaller ultra-marathons I've competed in, have I encountered anyone who said they wish they'd done less hill work. To complete a race like this you will need strong legs for those hills but you will also require a lot of mental reserves. Digging deep into these reserves is very rewarding when you eventually come out of the other end. Bigger and better than before. James Adams (British ultrarunner and author) said that the point of an ultra may be to break you down to small pieces that are then reconstituted to become greater than the sum of the parts. Meaning it can feel pretty terrible during the event but you emerge bigger, stronger and somehow better. A philosophy reminiscent of Nietzsche

Imagine the emotions you will feel as you emerge victorious like a latter day gladiator, from the darkness of despair to the triumphant sounds and cheers of the vibrant waiting gathered throngs, assembled from far and wide to mark and celebrate your emotional journey. Winston Churchill is supposed to have said:

"When you are going through hell. Keep going."

To complete the race well and finish with a good position you will need to be in very good physical shape indeed.

You've just run, stumbled and staggered forty miles in the last couple of days and the sun is beating down. The rays seem to pierce right through your skin and it feels like your organs are starting to glow. Your pack is chafing your shoulder and the red raw skin is somehow slippery. You wonder if it is blood.

The back of your t-shirt is sodden and cold. All clammy and lightly chilled to the touch. You try to recall the physics behind the latent heat of evaporation, but your brain swims out of focus and keeps going fuzzy around the edges. You kick yet another small black rock and stumble as it scuttles and skitters away. Cursing, you feel the stinging pain of the blood blisters under your nails. Part of you vaguely wonders if it might be a Thursday. You never could get the hang of Thursdays.

Just as you start to close in and gain ground on that old looking French chap just up ahead, him with the deep tan, grey hair and the wrinkles of a loosely fitting birthday suit, the slope increases. You

raise your head and glance up to see the path ahead winding out of sight as it meanders up and away between two alien looking outcrops of ancient orange rock. The wind whistles down the dusty gap between them like a hot hand harshly pushing you backwards. Just for malevolent fun it funnels dust swirls at your eyes making them all gritty. You gulp another swig of water past sun-baked rimy lips and vaguely wonder why you still feel thirsty despite drinking litres of the stuff. You think about chomping down a salt capsule and try to remember if it time to eat yet.

The slope gets the better of you and you lapse back into a walk. But that's not too bad. You tell yourself that each painful footstep is taking you ever closer to a large inflatable teapot and a lovely cold shower. Actually there isn't going to be a shower. Just a square of hot dusty carpet on a rather lumpy desert floor.

Are you a well rounded person?

How fat are you?

I'm not being mean, I can't see you and I don't care. The exact answer doesn't even matter that much. But it can matter a little bit. What does matter is, if you could be trimmer - what can you do to achieve this? How long have you got to prepare?

For every pound of fat which separates your physique from that of an elite international athlete, I invite you to think of this wobbly yellow pound (fat is sloshy, slimy and yellow under the skin) in two ways:

One - *you have to carry this with you and that can become rather tiring and a little tiresome. You will carry it up and down a lot of hills, you will haul it across a lot of sand. You will probably wish at some points that you weren't carrying quite so much of it around.*

Two - *this pound of unnecessary flesh contains 3500 calories worth of energy. This is a lot of energy which you don't need. The food you carry is compulsory, you really don't need all these extra energy stores. If you have seven extra pounds on board, this is* *enough energy to power you through an entire MdS.*

The number 3500 can be helpful to consider as you can then calculate realistically how much you can lose and how to do it. Having seven days in a row with a net energy deficit of 500 calories per day would do the trick nicely. That works out with a one pound loss each week. Though this would require a steady effort and no days for excuses.

Running more and only eating the same is a very efficient way of managing to lose some of our excess energy stores. By eating the same, I also hope this means swapping your snacking for more natural carbohydrates, cutting out most fatty and all processed foods, minimising the alcohol and swapping crisps and chocolate for fruit and vegetables.

If you would like to read a little more on weight losing stuff I can of course recommend my book the 'Skinny Genes' (a shameless plug, I know), though I will share quite enough in these few pages for you to sort yourself out (if like me there is a little sorting or streamlining that could perhaps be done as part of your MdS race preparation). You don't have to do anything of the sort of course, the emphasis here on our curvy middles is simply because if you are trimmer, you will feel better. If we feel better, the rest of life just seems to go an awful lot more smoothly.

Sleeping under the stars

Star filled nights in a far away place, far from the pollution of the cities and away from the stresses and strains from our busy daily lives and ever growing lists of things to do. There is something very splendid about being part of an experience like the MdS. It is so far removed from most of our day jobs that it can leave a deep lasting impact on many of its competitors.

Being under canvas, lying on a small piece of carpet on the desert floor, under a sky brim-filled with milky bright twinkling starlight, is a lovely thing to be part of. A thousand or so like-minded individuals from every corner of the globe assemble after each stage in this bizarre mini-city, which appears out of nowhere and which vanishes into thin air the next day leaving no trace. This city of many different nations and tongues all sharing a common goal, is surprisingly life affirming. It is a real privilege to be part of that experience, which is dramatically unique in its way to experience part of our amazing planet.

Treading lightly on the planet

The organizers of desert marathons are very keen you should embrace an environmentally oriented approach. **Tread lightly on the planet not leaving marks**, is the prevailing ethos. No littering, no phones in camp and biodegradable rustling brown poop bags are the order of the day. It part of the spirit of the event that it moves towards ecological sustainability. Each year more and more of the power used in the camp is solar powered. It is a special thing to be part of an event in an area of the world which isn't very touched, mired or marred by so-called civilization.

There is a splendid feeling you get when you are atop a dune in the scorching sunshine. Summiting after a lung bursting climb, with air rushing in and out in breathy gasps. Smiling in eager anticipation of a much welcome, albeit short downhill section as get to career down the steep side. All the while, in these moments of your sandy journey with no one else in sight and being so very far from your daily life back home. In these moments you experience part of the planet which humans haven't yet altered. The feeling is quite simply breathtaking. It is exhilarating, filling you with deep joy and an appreciation for just being alive. This can strike at you to your very core.

two

Entering

Many desert marathons outsell their places, with many applicants turned away. The Marathon des Sables, the famous race of the sands is easier to enter than to complete. To enter, you need to go online, fill out a form, pay a chunk of money and then join a long waiting list. Places often sell out in the first hour.

Most races have online applications now. Entering the MdS is different for different people depending where you live in the world. I found that some countries have shorter waiting lists than the United Kingdom (UK), which is heavily oversubscribed year after year. Each country has an allocated number of entrants The organizers are French, so the French do very well out of this arrangement. The race is very popular in the UK and there are only a couple of hundred places for us Brits. I wondered if I lived in a smaller less densely populated country, if my chances of being accepted would be higher. Unfortunately for me, I didn't have a postal address which I could use in Burkina Faso or the Solomon Islands - I like to think they would have accepted my application just out of curiosity if I had. The organizers do seem justifiably proud of the number of different nations involved each year.

Living in the UK, the entering process usually involves putting your name down for entry two or three years in advance. Sometimes during or just after some brave talk in a bar, possibly with your sound mind and sensible judgment a little impaired by the alcohol that you had just drunk. The places each year sell out in the first hour. Though do not despair of this, you can get yourself added to a waiting list for years that are already full. If you enter with a team you get an easier entry (you are a little more likely to be accepted for your chosen year), but you have to contend with the challenge of trying to coordinate a number of other people and you have to make sure that too many of the team don't pull out.

Many pull out in the lead up to the race for a variety of reasons. Many who enter as a team change their mind. I think this is because they are put off by the rule which states that you have to run three-legged with your ankles tied to your team-mates. Actually, I made that part up. Despite not having to race three-legged it can still prove logistically challenging to coordinate more than one person, as people may change their mind about entering because their life changes - their partner may object, they may have a baby, they may change their work commitments, they may get cold feet (once you are there, cold feet seems to be less of an issue). They may find that the training commitment is too big a project to embark on.

People tend to find their life goals evolve and when the time comes to pay the hefty entry fee, it suddenly doesn't seem quite tempting a prospect as it did during that drunken conversation down the pub.

The MdS is not cheap. The race does cost what for most competitors is rather a lot of money. There are without doubt cheaper races out there. There are even other races which offer desert racing for half the price (Kalahari being a great choice). However, the three and a half thousand plus pounds that it currently costs for an entrant from the UK does provide a lot of things. If you can afford it you will probably feel that you get a decent amount of stuff in exchange for your hard earned pounds. The iconic status of the MdS in my mind is well placed. I know of a few who disagree and this is their valid opinion. For me, I'd go again in a heartbeat.

My wife has on occasion pointed out that the race cost more than I tend to tell other people. She estimates that it costs several thousand more than the actual fee in add-ons you might not consider.

The logic goes as follows; by the time I'd spent a King's ransom on new and exotic ultra-lightweight kit, by the time I'd spent weekends away (in cheap hotels, mind you) to enter races around the UK in training, by the time all the preparatory race fees and traveling were included, by the time the expensive dehydrated special food and experiments with all varieties of sports nutrition were taken into account, that I'd spent many thousands of pounds over the actual entrance fee.

She also mentioned as she smiled, tight-lipped through gently gritted teeth with not a little chagrin, that I'd spent more on the MdS than I'd ever spent on a holiday for the pair of us. I tell you this only as a helpful hint. A heads-up notice to assist your strategy. It may take a little careful negotiation with your family to be allowed to go. Get the Brownie points in nice and early. It is well worth it. It is a great race to go and do.

We were all very well catered for, looked after, nuzzled and nurtured from the moment we arrived at Gatwick airport. We almost to a man (and woman) started with a game of I-spy. It was comparatively easy to play spot the MdS competitor in the airport. It seemed that they sported fresh haircuts, sporty outfits, the classic gaiter-look, funny hat and sunglasses. Inevitably they to a woman (and man) looked better trained, fitter, in superior shape and more of an athlete than myself.

At the check-in desk we met the MdS UK representatives in the flesh. We had become familiar with them by their postings on the internet forum, hosted on the book of faces. Additionally they had been in frequent contact by email over the previous months advising on what to take, insurance, race preparation and reminding us to badger our doctors for medicals amongst other things such and an ECG. We were assured that not being able to speak Arabic or Berber, the official languages in Morocco, would not be a problem. French was accepted as an unofficial language. Oh dear, my schoolboy French left a little to be desired. I would try to smile, shout louder in English and wave my arms a lot.

Then, just like a package holiday to somewhere hot and sunny, the cheery rep waved us into our first queue of many and we boarded our specially charted jet. We flew over France and Spain. We crossed the Straits of Gibraltar and on over the African continent. We passed the huge port of Casablanca, which presumably started life as a single white house.

We crossed the magnificent Atlas mountains and saw the edge of the Sahara. The Sahara is the third largest desert in the world after the colder ones at the poles. It turns out that it doesn't have to hot to be a desert as I had previously assumed. To be a desert it simply means that there isn't much rain. Not much rain at all, which renders it inhospitable to lots of the life we find elsewhere on this planet.

Desert comes from the Latin *desertus*, which means 'laid waste'. You don't need to call it 'the Sahara desert' as the name comes from the Arabic for 'the great desert'. This great desert stretches to cover most of North Africa and is similar in size to China or the United States of America. Here we were, descending from a clear blue sky to go and run around in it, like children arriving for the first day of a beach holiday. I had neglected to bring my bucket and spade.

On arrival at Ouarzazate airport (pronounced *wa-zah-zat*), a small hut in the dust with no vending machines in sight, we were bundled into coaches to transfer to the hotel which seemed to be a mere five minute drive away. The hotel for us UK runners was five stars of Moroccan luxury with banquet style buffets. We were well fed for a day and then transported by comfortable air conditioned coaches away from civilization, armed with generous sized packed lunches and the first of many, many litre and a half bottles of water.

The food before and after the race was surprisingly nice for mass catering in a desert. The organizers were French, so true to the expected stereotype of enticing cuisine and relaxed dining, there was even beer or wine included. The race had about one medic for every ten entrants, hundreds of them - this fantastic army of welcoming and much welcome volunteer support was distributed at checkpoints during the race itself and in a makeshift hospital tent at the end of each day.

To supplement the army of medics there were support crews nearly everywhere you looked, there were support helicopters, a plane and many roving safety vehicles. I felt that despite the marriage-testing price tag that I had decent value for the money I paid.

Passports and insurance

Each desert marathon has differing requirements. For the MdS, your passport needs to have a minimum of six months of validity on the day of departure. No visa is needed. When you arrive in Morocco and when you depart, you have to fill out immigration cards. These take a few minutes to complete and there don't really seem to be enough pens to go around. I recommend having a pen in your pocket for traveling. The airline too have their obligatory feedback cards so they can sell on all of your details to marketing companies.

Take a couple of pens with you for the journey to fill out boarding cards, customs cards, cards to enter the Morocco, cards to leave Morocco. It is partly the filling out of this stream of cards that made the queues slower than they needed to be.

You need to think about and purchase insurance cover. This could do with being able to cover cancellation should the need arise through unforeseen circumstances. The cover should extend to medical expenses and even international emergency evacuation.

I used the company called dog-tag as they seemed to provide a reasonable range of cover for what I determined to be a reasonable price-tag. It is worth noting that a number of travel insurance policies have exclusions for extreme events such as the Marathon des Sables. It could be helpful to go through your existing policy and look at the exclusions.

Monies

You need to carry cash (200€). This is for emergencies, such as if the need arises to get yourself back to civilization early, during the week.

When I raced, there are the expected opportunities to buy souvenirs, general tat and race goodies. These appear at Ouarazate initially in and around the hotel. There are tobacconists, several small supermarkets and the hotels themselves.

When on the coaches to and from the race proper, there are stops for toileting and for packed lunch eating. At these stops there are small local boys who appear from nowhere on foot, bicycle and on small ancient looking mopeds. They talk enthusiastically in broken English learned from films, to judge from the phrases and American accents.

Touting their crude jewelery, dodgy watches and scavenged fossils from the local region. While I had no desire for their goods I did have to admire their entrepreneurship and attitude to a business opportunity. The ammonites and trilobites are more plentiful out in the desert proper, but you may not wish to deliberately add the weight of a rock - albeit a historically ancient and debatably beautiful one, to your race-pack. When they are purveying these goodies you will still have your suitcase with you and they could be put in there for collection once you are victorious, at the week end.

Logistics & photographers

Differing races provide differing levels of support and catering. During my race the support on the race was incredible, enthusiastic, helpful and reassuring. The efficiency of the organization was truly amazing. Noticeably its timing, punctuality and anything requiring a watch was suitably laid back and relaxed. Yet despite this everything was achieved, with the minimum of fuss. A logistical *tour-de-force*. Very appropriate for the desert setting, very suitable for a hot and sunny holiday and really rather relaxing. It made a nice change from the rather unpleasantly frenetic pace of work back at home.

Professional photographers abound at the MdS. They make their money by selling their photographs to us, the competitors and to the press agencies of the world. Most, if not all, offer various packages. For example, a certain number of photographs showing you in camp and terrain throughout the event for a certain fee.

The prices range from a few hundred to a few thousand pounds. The photographers will probably be more focused on high end commissions and what he or she can sell via media rights and similar money driven motivations. If you aren't in the front half of the pack, there may be less value in commissioning a photographer as they will be less likely to capture your images as you pass.

What is an E.C.G.?

You will need an electrocardiograph (ECG) taken during the previous 30 days before the race start, before you are allowed to run in the Marathon des Sables.

An ECG (in the United States they use the German and give cardio a 'k' - EKG) is a tracing of the electrical output of your heart. Six sticky pads on the chest and one on each limb are wired to a machine which spews out a pretty piece of paper covered with tiny pink graph squares and a bunch of squiggly black lines. From these lines some clever doctors can figure out which heart conditions you may or may not have. Heart attacks and the classical changes seen when the heart is under strain can show up, along with some conditions that can cause sudden death.

Potentially avertable deaths are what the MdS medical team are keen to pick up before they let us loose in the sand. This is not entirely unreasonable. You will need an up to date ECG while the more senior amongst us are encouraged to get a quiet one plus one after exercise (to see if any ischaemic changes show up. These are caused by having not enough oxygenated blood going around the system).

* * *

Sudden death in young and apparently fit people does happen. The sort of things that cause sudden death in the young (and not so young) and otherwise fit, are conduction abnormalities where the electrical pulses and the wiring don't work properly. Your doctor will be on the lookout for any sign of these. He or she will examine the ECG carefully for any abnormal rhythm (hopefully yours will show no heart block and will hopefully beating along nicely in normal sinus rhythm and at a normal rate). The doctor will also look for your heart axis - which way it's 'pointing' (if the heart muscle is growing wonky or asymmetrically due to a valve problem or hole in the heart, this can show up here).

The heart of an athlete may be enlarged, as it grows with use just like any other muscle. Some left axis deviation and some left ventricular hypertrophy (when the biggest heart chamber is enlarged) is to be expected if we've done huge amounts of training. Some sinus bradycardia is expected too - which is the name for a slow resting heart rate (a slow pulse rate like that found in Olympic standard athletes, as low as 40 they tell me). Disappointingly for me, my resting heart rate only just dipped below 60 after many months of grueling training. On my pre-race ECG it was a magnificent 72. As this number in many people is a marker of their general fitness and a low number is a general badge of honor among athletes, I was gutted. Very sad for me indeed. On reflection, I should probably have eaten fewer pies.

Marathon runners can have really unhealthy hearts. Interestingly one can have quite badly furred arteries and be capable of running competitive marathons. It is a myth that marathon runners cannot have heart disease. Just being fit enough to get round is not a reassurance that all is well.

Always consult your doctor if you have chest pains, dizziness, unusual sweatiness, jaw ache or chest tightness. It is better to be safe than sorry. My youngest patient with a heart attack (myocardial infarction or MI) was only 22 years old. That having said - running and running very long distances leads to huge proven health benefits and at least delays heart problems in nearly everyone. This is of course very welcome and splendid news for those of us off to the Sahara for five or six very sandy, hilly marathons any time soon.

The biggest sudden silent killer in the fit is the partly inherited condition of hypertrophic obstructive cardiomyopathy (HOCM). This condition is where the dividing chunk (septum) running up the middle of the heart grows to be much thicker than is ideal. This septum is where the conduction wiring sits, so funny rhythms (arrhythmias) can happen, which is never a good thing. These arrhythmias can make the owner of this heart feel rather unwell. This unwellness may be very serious, including in some the heart actually stopping.

Hoping to spot this potential killer is why multi-million pound or dollar costing premiership footballers, American footballers or baseball stars always have their hearts checked out on transfer day. After all, you wouldn't want to spend all that money to find out that you'd bought a dud with a limited shelf-life.

Warning signs that patients may show of this potentially fatal condition include chest pain on exertion, giddiness on severe exertion and unexplained fainting or collapse (especially after exercise). There may also be the telltale signs on the ECG of right heart strain, conduction abnormalities and excessive left ventricular hypertrophy (that's just technical detail). This is one of the main conditions that those nice French doctors will be on the lookout for when we're all queued in the sand on a sunny afternoon at the beginning of April in the Southern Moroccan Sahara.

Try not to panic. You will probably not have something

seriously wrong. For all the precautions, the conditions looked for are actually really pretty rare and the rigmarole of producing an ECG will largely be a formality for most of us. Your General Practitioner (GP) will detect these problems when they look at your ECG before you leave. I appreciate the logistics of getting an ECG could be viewed as a hassle but it is compulsory. I think it is sensible and well worth it.

It also presents an excellent excuse to badger your GP and ask about any other niggles or technical questions you have. Though I should warn you, very few of my colleagues properly understand running and running injuries, they may not be familiar with our moans and groans (and probably won't know the word '**ultra**' in a running context). Accordingly, you should garner your advice from as many recommended sources as you can muster.

three

Training

Before you fly to the sun and sand for your amazing race, in could be sensible to give some thought to what it is that you want from the experience. If you want to enjoy the sunshine and revel in meeting amazing people from all four corners of the globe, then some of the details on training and kit won't really apply to you. Lots of people enjoy the race without a huge amount of training.

Many turn up with having not really run before, let alone having covered a marathon distance. I think a lot of the drop-outs and the casualties that limp like horror film extras across the camp each morning to climb aboard the bus (poor things, on those comfortable seats, with their coca-cola and their air conditioning) are likely to be among the less well prepared, though that's just an opinion.

I'm a little more obsessive that that. I wanted to achieve the above aims (enjoying and meeting all these amazing people, not the walking-like-a-zombie), but I wanted more. I wanted to push myself as hard as I could and see how I fared and measured up against other people. I'm a bit competitive like that and make no apology for this. I really enjoy all the detail and obsessing a little.

If this isn't your take on the MdS or indeed on life, that's absolutely fine. But as there is quite a lot of detail on training you might want to skip ahead a bit here!

The short version

The best way to train and improve is to get out of the door and do some miles. The best training for running is running. It is better to run off-road. Do at least one long run a week. Definitely take rest days. It is well worth doing some hills and it is worth doing one fast run a week. Eat sensibly and get enough sleep.

Training with a pack

This is a **really** good idea. But how fast and how much?

Desert racing for most runners outside the top 100 (and a few who are well inside) involves a significant chunk of walking. By a chunk I mean that people finishing about half way up or down the pack (depending on your point of view) should expect that they might be walking for nearly half of the event.

No matter how spritely you are up the local trail - when the sun is baking down, your back is soaked with sweat, your bruised feet sore, you cannot get a decent step because of the soft sand and then you have to shlep up a hill ...You are probably going to have to walk, at least a little.

- The more blisters you have - *the more walking you will do.*
- The more weight in your pack - *the more walking you will do.*
- The more weight in your pack - *the bigger your blisters.*
- The more puny your muscles - *the more walking.*

* * *

Wearing a heavy pack slows you down. Wearing a pack and trying to run feels different. The pack moves. The pack bounces. The pack rubs.

Walking is slow - which in one way is nice because you get to enjoy the scenery and you can correctly reason this provides better value for money as you are on the course for longer. After about five hours of enjoying the scenery in fifty or so degrees of Saharan sun, I for one was more than happy to admit that I wanted to be back on my piece of magic carpet, in the shade in the luxurious surroundings of my tent.

Bivouac is of course the correct term for this tent thingy. Bizarrely on the MdS they were black. Black absorbs heat and light making them hotter during the hot sunny days and colder during the cold dark nights. I learned all of this years before at school during physics lessons. I never did come to understand the reasoning behind this obviously poor color choice for the cloth of our tents. I mean bivouacs.

So, I hear you cry - *how can I haul myself round a bit quicker?*

This is a good question and I'm glad you asked. The answer lies in good preparation and in attention to detail. It may also help to stick to a bunch of the general principles that I've packed into this handy guide eagerly clutched in front of you.

Weight, weight, weight. Your weight, your **pack** weight, the weight of your **cuddly toy** mascot and the weight of the **water** you carry all matter. Making a judgment call of which items to take along with you is tricky and will vary between people depending on all sorts of things.

- Less is definitely more here.

* * *

The less weight you are carrying, the more efficient every single step you take will be, the less time you will take, the less water you will need - if you're quick enough around the course you don't even have to drink all the water. I carried and drank about a third less water than most people and will tell you more about that later.

Surrounded by runners on all sides you haul yourself forward. Feeling the stiffness in your quads, you leave the start line behind. The helicopter swoops so low you can't hear the shouts of those right next to you. People call to their friends in a cacophony of languages. Different accents all swooping past your ears. Dust and sand blows up around you making progress sluggish. Like a slug.

Your heavy leaden feet shuffle up and down the small tussocks. Some of these crested with scrubby desert plants. The bastard bushes. You concentrate harder, trying not to catch your gaiters on the razor sharp thorns. Your steps are accompanied by the rhythmic sloshing of your water bottles as you stumble onward.

Slipping and sliding a little with every step, you try to run in the firmer packed vehicle tracks, despite the sand kicked up by the other runners. It seems as though there are about seven hundred in front of you and you wonder how many of these you will see again and perhaps overtake as the day goes on. The sun didn't seem too hot while you were in the starting pen, but shuffling forward it seems as though someone just turned the heating dial up to eleven. Breathless and thirsty you check your watch, you've only been going ten minutes.

Cold weather training

If you are preparing for this fifty degree centigrade sandy desert challenge in the UK, Europe or the United States and haven't given yourself more than six months to train, you may well have a weather challenge. My race was in April, and the preceding months in the Northern hemisphere are most definitely on the wintry side.

I live in very green pleasant surroundings. There is a reason the vegetation is lush and verdant, this is because it rains. A lot. It rains especially a lot in the winter. Snow would have been better for my training because at least that feels underfoot a bit like sand. Although you can usually feel your toes when you are running on the sand. In fact, when you can feel your toes while on this sand, sometimes you may wish you couldn't because this means you can also feel pain.

The four months of my main training also had to be fitted around a sixty hour working week through this inconvenient winter. I was determined to get daily training in, though this meant a tight schedule. Up at five, leave for my run at half five after a pint of water and a bathroom stop. Run for about an hour, try to thaw out a little, put wet smelly kit into the washing machine, bung porridge into the microwave, shower, shave, leave for work after doing the teeth and ironing a shirt. At this point it was still dark.

Get back from work at seven or so in the evening (again, this was dark), have some scoff, wave at my long-suffering better half, flop onto the sofa, crash into bed, rinse and repeat for four to five months. This sort of schedule is challenging enough to do, but it can prove more testing for your loved ones. These loved ones may not actually be as excited about the race as you. These sort of issues may need to be borne in mind, as they could lead to relationship tension.

My poor wife used to wake up at the same time as me because of my loud alarm clock and not be able to get back to sleep. She didn't have the race to look forward to, or to focus on. She didn't gain any of the health benefits I got from the exercise and experienced none of my endorphins. I'm supremely grateful to her for supporting me far more than I realized at the time. It is also perhaps worth bearing in mind that the MdS is interesting to hear about for most people. But probably only for a minute, tops. I exceeded on many occasions the social acceptability of this niche topic. I have to apologize to my remaining few friends for this oversight.

Four, forty five. The alarm clock rings. Jerking me out of slumber and I start to surface. Mentally searching for the place where consciousness kicks in. I break though and waken with a jolt. Cautiously peering out through half eyes like a hedgehog in a bright but brisk Spring morning facing into a stiffening breeze. With an effort I open my eyes more fully and try to remember …Remember why.

I reach for the phone and try to silence the alarm. It takes me several attempts in the cold air which stings at my semi-numb nose.

I try not to disturb my silent wife as I summon up the courage to swing the legs out. Mind over mattress. Beat the hypnotic seductive power of the duvet. I'm up and on my way to the bathroom. Undies, running tights and heart rate monitor. T-shirt and socks.

Quick pee, slip on my running watch and then downstairs. Big glass of water and start some warm up exercises. I try to get some life into my limbs at five in the morning. The hour feels so unnatural. Like I'm the only person on earth who is awake. This is clearly rubbish, but the morning air is quiet and still. Off then to the bathroom for my toilet visit. I'm hoping my stiff limbed movements have got the bowels working. I hate having to answer the call of nature while I'm out running.

Fluorescent hi-viz jacket, warm hat and MP3 player on. I fill my water bladder and check the sand bags (dishwasher salt) in my pack. I shrug the heavy load up onto my shoulders and fit the headlight. Turn off the lights, check the cats haven't wandered out on to the road and head out of the door. Just before quarter past five. I slip my warm waterproof gloves on. It's time to jog.

The wind whips the light rain into bright swirling sparkles which dance in the bright searchlight beam of my headlight. All the street lights are off at this early hour. Not a soul moves out in the early December morning. Time for a quick six mile loop before work. I tell myself that all these efforts will pay off when it comes to the dunes.

I wonder how different it will feel to be too hot for a change, as I try to generate some heat of my own by running a little faster. The pack bouncing around on my back makes moving more challenging than it needs to be on the slippery pavement.

The UK winter training was typically so cold that I wore a waterproof and windproof jacket, a buff to cover my neck, running tights, warm waterproof gloves and a woollen beanie hat on every run for five months until I left for Morocco. It was below freezing for most of these runs and often raining. As I gazed excitedly out at the disappearing Gatwick runway, it was fitting that heavy snow was falling.

Training for desert marathons may be considered under the following headings:

- Training your muscles for endurance
- Training your brain for endurance
- Improving your VO2 max
- Improving your running efficiency
- Strengthening your muscles
- Strengthening your core
- Managing your weight
- Training for the terrain
- Training with your gear

Endurance muscle training

Endurance is the ability to run for longer. You get better at running long distances and better endurance mainly by running longer distances.

Your muscles have fast twitch fibers and slow twitch fibers. If your muscles are stuffed with fast twitch fibers you will be better at explosive movements such as those used for tennis, sprinting and soccer. If your muscles are stuffed mainly with slow twitch fibers you may well be better at long distance running, endurance cycling and the longer swimming and rowing disciplines.

You are born with a certain proportion of each type of muscle fiber. This means it is genetically pre-determined if you will be more of a sprinter or more of an endurance runner or someone with abilities right down the middle. Despite being born with a predominance in one field, nearly everyone can steer their muscles towards one end of the extremes or the other by specific types of training. There are also thought to be fibers that lie dormant (undecided whether they would like to be fast or slow) and these are engaged by training.

Running distances of marathon length are going to need a lot of these slow twitch endurance fibers. Training a muscle to perform over the many hours a marathon takes, results in changes at the level of the individual cells. The fiber bundles actually become bigger with this training. The cross-linkages between the contracting parts of the muscles become more numerous (meaning they contract faster and with more force). The amount of calcium released at each contraction increases making the contraction more powerful and the movement more efficient.

The powerhouses of the cell, the mitochondria, vastly increase in number in muscles which are worked. When these numbers go up, there is more energy available to the muscle fibers. This is one of the main features which improves in a muscle trained for endurance. These adaptations can take about six weeks or more. It takes this long because there are many changes which have to happen in the muscle cells and these are too complex to happen quickly. You probably need to run consistently three times a week to notice obvious improvements. These improvements in your endurance can be noticed much sooner than the six weeks your body takes to make the full extent of the changes and this can spur motivation to continue the training.

We have just passed the twenty mile mark. Leaving the aid station with its comforting friendly smiling faces feels almost painful. The hearty congratulations from the stalwart volunteers stood out on the cold felt good to hear. Standing there in the January freezing rain to welcome us weary travelers, their efforts were greatly appreciated. The hills were harder than I remember from last year. Another twelve miles to go on the first day of Pilgrim Challenge. Twelve more miles of slipping around in the mud.

My thighs are on fire and my pace has dropped to a slow shuffle. I had set off initially rather ambitiously with the pack of lead men and held their pace for the first ten miles. Proper runners. This was clearly a mistake and now I'm paying dearly for those early fast miles. My body has hit the wall, and running feels like I am wading through treacle. Looking at the huge chunks of mud, grass and other parts of the North Downs Way making an inch thick coating on my shoes, it looks a bit like treacle too.

I scoff down a sausage roll and gulp at an ice cold glass of water. Throw the cup into the trash and head off down the trail. These are the times when you learn stuff about yourself. I don't usually find very much to inspire me, just stuff to moan and whinge about. Luckily I manage a smile and a thank you as I leave. In a few metres with this weather, no one will hear me as I complain about the mud and no one will see the faces I pull as I drag my sorry butt down the gentle slope. I'm still in the top twenty at this stage and if only I can warm up a bit and get some food, in I could still finish well. This motivation will help I know, but coordinating my cold stiff fingers is proving tricksy.

Later tonight I will be wrapped up in layers and layers of warm clothes. Basking in the achy limbed smugness of having finished an ultramarathon in the sort of weather that has everyone else (everyone sensible?) curled up on their sofa inhaling potato chips and beer. The shared experience that binds everyone in the food queue later, together in unspoken camaraderie will give me a buzz while I await my huge plate of steaming yummy food. This spurs me forward. I soldier on. I wouldn't really rather be anywhere else, despite the temporary moaning about the discomfort that is lost forever, carried away on the wind. No one hears.

Training your brain for endurance

Your brain is quite clever. Without any conscious thought it does lots of clever stuff. But your brain can slow you down. Your brain will hold back your sports performance so you don't become injured.

In our ancestors this would have been a life preserving safety feature. While racing, this can be a mild inconvenience. Putting your body through grueling experiences teaches it the next time it experiences these, that things aren't so bad and it is likely to pull through. Having the brain learn through adversity will allow it to unleash resources to allow you to carry on rather than quit whenever the going gets a bit tough. Well, so the theory goes.

In addition to the brain part that acts on the muscles, the psychological benefit of previous exposure to tricky stuff gives you mental reserves that you can draw on when you are struggling. In the desert, you may well struggle at times. There will be quite a lot of challenges when the going gets sandy.

Lots of races exist in which you can challenge your metal. There are many such events in the UK that offer this chance to test and push your physical endurance and to push your mental side too. These are well worth attending. I can particularly recommend the Coastal Trail Series by the EnduranceLife team. Along with any of the XRNG events, particularly the Pilgrim's Challenge at the end of January. Miles and miles of hills and mud. Dirty weekend fun for everyone.

Improving your VO2 max

VO2 max is the maximum delivery of oxygen to the muscles. It is the power output of the whole system, a measure of your cardiovascular fitness, a surrogate marker.

Your cardiovascular fitness is a measure of how efficiently your heart and lung package can get oxygenated blood to your muscles. When you train this component, your heart grows in size, every beat becomes more efficient, your circulating blood volume goes up, you make more red blood cells and the size and number of blood vessels in your muscles increases too. These are all good things. The more intensively you train the better from this point of view, as it all improves.

The fastest and the biggest improvements occur when you train at a high intensity. Your genetics will determine your upper VO2 max and undoubtedly some people have a natural genetic advantage. Most runners operate nowhere near what they can achieve. Most of us can haul ourselves up by about twenty with some well directed training. For example, the average couch potato could score 25, a jogger 40, a club runner 55 with the internationals at about 65 plus and the world class superstars at 75 to 80.

* * *

Improved cardiac output happens with training. The muscle changes which happen in the muscles of the body also happen in heart (cardiac) muscle. The fibers get bigger, they contract better and overall efficiency is increased. There is no change in fast or slow twitch fibers though, as the heart has none. This is because the heart is made from smooth muscle as opposed to the striated (stripy looking under a microscope) muscle of everywhere else and this smooth muscle (amazingly) never becomes tired.

The maximum speed and effort that you can run will be able to be maintained for only a few seconds. The more seconds you can spend at this level of effort, the quicker your body will change and adapt. This is what interval training is all about. Repeated sprints at maximal effort with short periods of recovery help increase your performance level. This increase in performance lasts for weeks and months even if you don't use it. These changes happen quickly and are noticed within a week or two.

There are two popular ways of doing sprint training. One is to sprint and then fully recover so you aren't short of breath. Then off you trot for another sprint after you've allowed yourself to rest. The second way is to sprint, then before you are fully recovered you try again, repeating these intervals without recovery. Probably the very best training will involve alternating these two as each will probably give you slightly different benefits.

One speed session a week is about right. Hill sessions can provide an alternative to sprint sessions if you want some variety in your training. This is because the leg power and increased cardiac output needed to power you up a hill is much the same as all out efforts on flatter surfaces. Be sure to give it all you've got on the way up and then jog back down for another go, using either of the above methods.

* * *

When you increase your VO2 max you become a more efficient runner. You go faster, you can go further, with less effort and burn less fuel along the way. It is, in short, some of the very best training you can do.

Improving your running economy

Your running economy is how well and how efficiently you move. This is how much forward movement you get for a certain amount of effort. The better the economy, the further you can go on a certain amount of fuel and you increase how long it takes you to hit the wall, if you hit it at all.

Running a lot will help. Fast running will help a lot more. The way to become more efficient is to get more out of each movement. Good strong legs to brace your landing will help. A well toned core and an upright posture will help too. If you aren't sure if you have a good posture, then holding your head nice and high while looking out about twenty meters in front of you should help a little. And of course buy my forthcoming book on posture 'Stand Up, Sexy'

Increasing your range of motion will improve your running economy. If you warm up and down properly and stretch well, then your muscles will be as limber as they can be. This will give you a good range of motion. This range can further be improved by careful daily stretching and yoga-like exercises.

Strengthening your muscles

Working at your muscle strength is about using them a lot and taking plenty of protein in your diet. Aim to have two grams of protein for each kilogram you weigh, each and every day you are working on your muscles. And on the rest days.

You can either work your muscles by weights and machines at the gym, or out doing proper running. Simply running fast will do it well. If you can, run up and down hills. If you can do this fast, then this will be even better. Doing this off-road on slippery and on uneven surfaces will train you well.

Lifting bigger weights will bring bigger, better results. If you are not in the gym, this means plyometrics (the word for explosive movements). Such as jumping jacks, mountain climbers, box jumps and so on. You tube will help you out if these terms are new to you.

Doing squats is probably the single best gym exercise for running if you only have it in your heart and enthusiasm to perform one. You don't have to do too many reps. But squat with the absolute heaviest weight you can manage. You will improve fastest if you push your limits here three times a week, though I do acknowledge this might not be a practical option for you. Good technique is vital when using heavy weights and most gyms will have a friendly instructor or other gym user to ask. They love to be asked for advice and tips. It makes them feel important and you get help and assistance. Win win.

Strengthening your core

The core is a term used to describe a whole lot of muscles which work in close harmony with one another as an effective single unit. Your tummy muscles (abdominals), lower and upper back muscles, the paravertebrals next to your spine, your pelvic muscles and some of your buttock muscles are all involved. It is your core which helps you to sit and stand. If you have a good core you will run better because the arms and legs you swing about will have an excellent well-toned base from which to swing. One which doesn't pivot, rotate, flex, bend or twist too much.

Running on trails is really good for your core. There are core exercises you can do at home too. Press ups, sit ups, crunches and planks are all excellent. Yoga and Pilates are great too. However, probably the best thing for your core is the simplest: **Perfect posture**.

Sitting up well and standing with a perfect erect posture are vital for core development and maintenance. They also have the advantage that you can work on them nearly anywhere, nearly all day and you don't even need to get changed. If you are doing them in the supermarket queue, you may like to try not to let it show in your face. People may assume you have some sort of medical problem. Possibly with your bowels.

Managing your weight

Improving your performance in most endurance sports is about improving your power to weight ratio. Running is very much about being as powerful as you can be for your weight. You want good strong muscles but not massive ones. You also need to be fairly low on the body fat percentage points. Your running will not be assisted if you are too cuddly around the middle. You thighs should not rub together too much when you run. If they do, your chafing challenges during your desert marathon are going to be worse than they need to be. Watching your food intake while increasing your training should result in steady progress towards your ideal body shape. Get started soon and keep up the good work.

Training for the terrain

Sandy work training would be ideal for desert marathon training. Sand and a lot of hills. Also somewhere with fairly uneven ground will come in handy. Your ankles and lower legs will soak up a lot of forces when you run on the uneven ground. These uneven forces will be magnified with your pack weight. During the race your footfalls on this uneven and soft terrain may well be being made with tired legs. I certainly ended up staggering around like a zombie. A drunk zombie with rickets. And a nasty case of painful haemorrhoids.

The more training you get to do off the flat (boring) roads and on the trails, the better. The more hill work you can get done, the better. Practice sprints up hills for not only your VO2 max, but for general strength and coordination uphill. In addition to running, consider practicing fast walking up hills for what you will actually be doing in the desert. As everyone can walk we mistakenly don't tend to think this needs practice.

In the desert you are going to be walking at some stage. If you want to finish the race as quickly as you can, practice the walking. Brisk walking with your full pac. The muscles you engage when fast walking differ from slow jogging. If you are well trained, alternating fast walking with jogging is an effective technique for covering the miles.

When you walk fast with a rapid foot turnover and fully engaging your muscles you can make considerable progress. Working on this in your training will help strengthen the muscle sets which you will use during the race and is probably worth the effort. Perhaps as often as weekly. You could even use this for one of your rest day's activities if you don't want to fully rest. Your tushy will know when you've had a decent walking session. Your buttocks will ache with delayed onset muscle soreness (DOMS) for the next couple of days. This is a pain in the ass, but a good one.

In addition to going up, most runners will also find useful gains from practicing their downhill technique. This is best worked on when you are already fit and strong. The way to descend well is to lean forward and either turn your legs over as fast as they can like tiny windmills or by taking long poweful strides to increase your speed. This will depend on the angle and grip you have.

If the slope is too steep, you should zig-zag like a skier. If the slope is covered in wet leaves, ice, scree or otherwise looks like traction is going to be a problem, then hunker down. Bring your weight down, pull your center of gravity closer to the floor with your arms held out for balance. With your bottom close to your heels you can then slide in a semi-controlled way, occasionally using a half run too. Watching fell runners will give you something to aim for in terms of style. There are also internet videos of Kilian Jornet who is one of the world's greatest ultra-runners today. His downhill technique is well worth emulating.

If you find yourself totally out of control on a descent and can't regain control by zig-zagging, I'm told you can jump. This sounds counter-intuitive. Apparently all you have to do is simply leap into the air, landing a metre or so away on better footing which allows you to regain control. I've not tried this in anger, but am happy to pass the tip on. Good luck and happy landings.

I will add a note here that although descending enormous sand dunes was my favorite part of the race, there is an important safety consideration. Your vertical speed down can be really quite fast and the soft sand is really forgiving, which is nice. However the desert floor at the base of the dune will be pretty much like landing on granite. You will be well advised to control and slow your descent before you hit the bottom at high speed. Perhaps by angling your run a little towards the end and just slowing your steps a little.

Training with your gear

Running in your special desert shoes, with gaiters, with your fully laden pack, with a hat, buff and two huge bottles of water and drinking bottles and an assortment of snacks can feel a little different to your normal running outfit. Add to that lot a flare, a road book, a transponder around your ankle or GPS device, a compass in your hand and you may well feel your running style changes a little too.

The gear you will wear for the race will differ from that of your typical training run. This is worth bearing in mind as the muscles you have trained may be a little different from the ones you use in the desert. The way your feet move, the way that they land and the way that your feet move about within your shoes may also be different in the desert. As small issues and niggles are magnified when you are hot and tired, it might benefit you to try and consider these in advance. Managing your outfit and training with it a little could turn out to be time well spent.

You may of course not run into any blisters, chafing issues, or any muscle aches and pains. This may be because you are well prepared or simply lucky. There are twelve hundred or so competitors at the MdS and a wide range of problems emerge to hamper people's race enjoyment and race progress. It was gratifying for me to not have problems to the same level and degree as some others. I think time spent in careful preparation pays off.

Road-runner

I'm not sure if this is going to come as a surprise to you, but: you will meet very little terrain during your desert marathon which resembles Tarmac.

If you train on Tarmac you will clearly therefore not be giving yourself the best terrain specific training advantage. There is going to be a lot of sand. The word around the camps is that in previous years there was more hard and rocky terrain on the events but now there is plenty of the sandy stuff. You can now reliably look forward to lots of this sand every day. This is a good thing as you do feel you get your money's worth.

Running on sand is a little different from other surfaces. Running on sand is tricky because the stuff moves about under your feet and you can't really get very good traction. The difference between grip or purchase from the outsole (underneath bit) of the different shoes probably doesn't make that much of a difference.

I was hoping for a competitive advantage by clever shoe selection. I had rather hoped the right shoe might prove more time efficient than doing more training (or the less palatable option of avoiding cake). After careful consideration, I elected to take with me fell-running shoes with an aggressive outsole (this means the lugs were quite chunky, which means that the rubber bits on the soles of the shoes were quite lumpy and sticky-outy). I used Inov8 x-talon 212s and would happily take them again. I usually wear a size seven and took this size with me without selecting a larger size, as seems to be widely touted on forums as *de rigeur*.

There isn't much cushioning in these shoes but I was ok with that as I'm quite used to running off-road on the trails with these. The chunky lugs helped quite a lot with taking the pain out of landing on hard sharp rocks. It may well be that the best shoes for nearly everyone will be the ones they already own and are used to. I didn't mind the lack of cushioning. The rocky descents in these were quite manageable.

I should mention my new found desert habit of kicking small and not so small rocks. I'm not sure how often you kick rocks back home, but there are a lot of rocks in that desert and I kicked a fair proportion of these. Steel toe capped boots at several points seemed like they could have been a better footwear choice. I'm sure you won't kick rocks. It's just my lack of technique. You wouldn't be that foolish I'm sure.

The sandy descents were simply amazing fun and almost worth the entry fee alone - quite my favorite part of the week by a long chalk. Running on sand for your training might not be quite as much fun as there is usually not quite enough of it. If you can find somewhere sandy to go and play, I highly recommend it. Practicing running on sand will build up your stabilizer muscles and core. Having your feet slipping sideways and otherwise having lousy traction involves stabilizer muscles and builds up your ligaments. Using a pack would bring even more benefit.

I appreciate not many people have access to sand. Snow is pretty good too. If you cannot get any sand or snow work, the next best thing is mud. There is usually plenty of this in the UK in Winter. I wish I'd done more work on muddy hills. I recommend simply using whatever trails you can find. You should also embrace as much hill work you can stand, I may have mentioned this. Core work won't go far amiss either. You probably can't do too much core work. Planks, mountain climbers, diagonal sit ups, heel raises and standard crunch sit-ups ...Every day. Well done you, I can feel your enthusiasm building already.

Can you train in the gym?

There are things you can do in the gym which will support your preparation. In an ideal world this does not include the treadmill. I appreciate this may be contentious. However, I believe using the treadmill can a really bad way to practice your running. There is no wind resistance, the floor is sprung and every step you take is identical which not only doesn't provide the stimuli your muscles and ligaments need to strengthen for the real world, but the identical repetitive action actually increases the risk of sustaining an injury because each impact is in exactly the same place.

This makes treadmill running not very realistic. I know for you there may be some very good reasons to run on the treadmill, but if you have a practical option not to, then get yourself out of that door. Trail running is a lot safer with fewer injuries for precisely the reasons that each footfall is different, there is wind resistance and there is lots of variety to how each and every foot lands. Even running on the pavement or road is better than the treadmill. A lot of enthusiastic gym users thought it was the other way around.

There are a few benefits of the treadmill such as safety from assailants and rabid dogs. Plus easy access to your locker, nice lighting, good music (questionable) and being warm and dry. If for you the cold and the dark is so off-putting that running on a treadmill is the only acceptable alternative to sitting on your sofa or in the bar, then do it.

If you feel you really have to use a treadmill, then to get the most out of it try wearing a pack, set the gradient to the max, crank up the speed and learn to power stride. This will at least build some great muscles to power you past people in the race. A considerable mental boost if you are a tiny bit competitive. You'll manage even more smug points if you can manage a smile, wave and a few words of encouragement. I do not know if these smug points are worth the funny looks you may get from other gym users.

The stepper at the gym is valuable piece of equipment. This will build your ability to zoom up hills. I'm sure you won't be surprised to hear I prefer using real hills. There are a surprising number of hills on the race. It seems at times that the race is mainly uphill. It always seems the wind is blowing in your face too. I do not know why this is. I suspect it may have been flatter than I perceived it and really I just wasn't strong enough.

Either way, using the stepper to build your butt and work on core muscles to support your posture will be great training. It is worth noting that to get the most out of the stepper; crank up the resistance and have a fast step turnover (cadence). Having a high step and a fast step will help you up the hills when you are up against it in the sandy stuff. Opinion is split between using either quick small steps or big lunging steps with your arms pressing on your quads for stability in hill climbing. I prefer short and fast, as I tend to get cramps from my weedy muscles with the other technique while racing. Pick the one which suits you and practice that.

* * *

After each work out, head to the mat for stretching and rollering. Think of this as part of the workout. I really believe for the best preparation that this stretching time on the mat is a worthwhile investment. Work your entire body through the stretches. These are more important, if like me, many years are in your past. Our muscles and ligaments stiffen up as the years pass. This isn't a good thing and increases injury risk. Stretching regularly and especially after exercise, decreases injury rate.

The average age of competitors at the Marathon des Sables is youthful forty one. There are lots of senior runners. *This isn't really a race that starts to appear on bucket lists and appeals to someone in the midst of a mid-life crisis. Uselessly railing against the relentless march of time, full of remorse at wasted younger years* ...Ok, maybe it is. **But** it is cheaper than a sports car and safer than buying a motorcycle.

The stationary bike in the gym (or the home, when it isn't covered in washing) can provide a nice change in your routine to provide variety. You may find using the bike works muscles which aren't primarily those that will be most helpful for you on the MdS. The notable exception to this is spinning classes. This fixed bike routine provides a good work-out to boost your sprint work, which will bring up your VO2 max. It is also a motivator to be in a group of others and you may well push yourself a little harder under this encouragement. This is something you may have noticed and one of the reasons that exercise classes of all types are so popular. There is good medical science to back this up too. Group sessions of any type of exercise have been shown to motivate male athletes to try harder for longer. In the ladies the effect is measurable but not nearly as significant.

Sport specific training

Opinion varies about how much and what type of cross-training to do.

When you train for a sport, the muscle groups you use the most will develop the most. The way you use your joints will affect how you develop strength around them. The supporting ligaments strengthen and coordination improvements develop which will be very specific to the activity you are performing. The motor groups within the muscles are enhanced and become more powerful. These muscle groups contract harder and more efficiently when trained. In addition, the nerves become more efficient. Through regular use, the neural pathways in your brain actually thicken and conduct nerve impulses better. These nerve pathway changes are enough to actually change the shape of your brain. These thicker nerve pathways work to power your muscles and body to make it more efficient.

These changes are all in response to repeated specific stresses. They take months and years to develop. This is the response to training. It is also why the benefits are not instant. This predictable training response is why the professionals do this a lot. Every day. Up to four times a day.

* * *

This training response is why Olympic champions are usually only very good at the sport they've trained for and aren't international standard at any other. Of course they are fit, strong and well coordinated but **sport specificity** is crucial if you want to compete at the very top of the game. This sport specificity is because the brain and the body physically change during the many hours of hard and carefully tailored training over years. The neural pathways in the brain are altered during training in such a way that makes it quicker and easier for the body to perform those actions you have rehearsed. The body changes are highly specific too. The muscle groups you use in the actions you perform in training are reinforced and made stronger.

The outcome of these changes are that when you train for one thing, you will get better. These changes won't however make you necessarily any better at other sport or activity. Weight lifters may not make very good ice skaters, gymnasts might not be great at the shooting and those who are excellent at sailing might not be quite so good at the marathon. This is useful to know, because if you want to be a great trail runner, you will have to work at trail running.

It is not necessarily a bad thing that working at one sport doesn't give you a free pass to be brilliant at all the others. These different and sometimes distinct changes which occur are good because they happen in a particular way which is very predictable. It is this very predictability we can take advantage of. Tailoring our training to maximize these changes. We can work on the very things which will help to make us better and more efficient at our chosen sport.

This explains why the world's elite athletes may be really rather average when turning their hand to something else outside their chosen arena. It is not that their skills, attitude, tenacity and dedication aren't transferable - it is because their bodies (and their neural pathways) are very well adapted for just the one thing.

Each sport requires different actions and muscles. Using your non preferred sport as part of a training regimen or regime is referred to as **cross training**. This is why cross training on something like a stationary bike will have limited benefits for someone who just wants to get better at running. The benefits of cross training do include it being a break from your usual training routine. A break which can be nice for the variety, along with a well earned rest for your joints from repetitive actions. Cross training can be beneficial but has its limitations. Knowledge of these pros and cons will better inform your choices.

There is a place for cross training in maintaining fitness while resting an injury. For example if your shins hurt you may still be able to cycle. While resting an injury, cross training can prevent you from going stir crazy with cabin fever. You may notice that if you can cycle but can't run, this hints they use different muscles and time on a bike may not make you a better runner. Some say cross-training stops you becoming bored of the same routes and routines.

Cross training can help while resting an injury so you don't lose all of your hard earned cardiovascular fitness. This starts to drop after a couple of weeks of not exercising and in highly trained individuals it can take three months to return to even the baseline fitness of the general population. So don't panic too much right away if you need a week off for injury, work or pressing social commitments. But don't leave it too long.

Cross training delivers key benefits to your core. Having a strong set of muscles around your middle is invaluable for running generally, but on uneven terrain wearing a heavy pack, being equipped with a rock solid core makes a huge difference to running economy and efficiency.

Being a more efficient runner feels nicer, moves you faster and hurts a lot less. In multi-day events, you finish faster and thus get more time to relax and recover. When indulging in other sports you take advantage of the way they these work your core differently to running, keeping your abdominals in good shape - definitely a good thing and highly beneficial to your running.

Cross training is not quite as good as actually doing a daily specific core work out - but few of us actually manage that. I don't enjoy it. Because my core isn't good enough, it hurts. So I tend to avoid it despite knowing how important it is!

My way of achieving some core work in is to play tennis once a week - which is fun and I enjoy the competition. Running is all a bit solo, often in the dark and I'm my only competition in the cold and the rain. Sadly I'm only too aware that the tennis isn't as good as a proper gym session, but I justify it to myself anyway.

Please do cross-train if you want to and enjoy it, but appreciate its limitations as well as its benefits. It is of course better for your body to be doing something rather that eating doughnuts on the sofa. Don't tire yourself out so you get less from your next running session. When you are tired, your injury risk goes up. Injuries sustained in this way are really unhelpful and unnecessary.

Tapering - what is a tapir?

A taper is something which burns and then fires a rocket up into the sky. It is also the period of rest and relaxation before a big race.

Tapering is all about resting the body and soul before a big race. The benefits in terms of muscle strength, coordination and endurance gained over your training over the preceding months and years took a while to accumulate. The last few weeks are much less important. Rest here will give more benefits than more training. Late efforts fall under the law of diminishing returns. That does of course assume that you've actually put these efforts in far enough in advance. And you have not left it all a bit late and last minute.

If you don't taper down, you run the risk of turning up at a race tired, not fresh and mentally exhausted. You might not sleep well before a big event and that on top of tired muscles will significantly decrease your chances of performing well. When you train tired, you also increase your injury risk.

One of my worries was the closer I got to the race, the more I worried about sustaining a silly injury like a sprained or broken ankle, a stress fracture or twisted knee. Nothing too significant, but enough to mean that I couldn't race in the MdS and thousands of pounds and many months of training out of the window.

I took about a month off before the race. I'm not entirely sure why, when I review various aspects of my preparation and how they measured up in the harsh daylight of the race. A whole month, on reflection was a bit too long. I used it to get in an hour or more of sauna time nearly every day for the three weeks before I left, which was nice but I suspect didn't help in the slightest.

I now wish I'd tapered my mileage down instead of virtually stopping it. I should have simply stopped the pack work as I was strong enough. One weight session a week, plus one easy paced long run of thirteen miles, one twenty minute hard hill session and one twenty minute fartlek sprint session. This would have been perfect for me. Clearly there will be many competitors who simply use their long run on a Sunday as the only training they do. Of course that is fine too. I'm not saying my suggestions are the only way to prepare for desert marathons. There will be plenty of runners at these events who are faster than me and will train harder. These tips are mainly for those front to middle of the pack runners who are curious about how to do a bit better. They are also only one voice and one opinion.

A note of caution if you drop your mileage - you don't need to eat as much! I put on several pounds in the last month and really regretted it. It was purely a lack of discipline and a feeling of general smugness at having achieved so much in the previous five months. It is crucial for an optimal strategy that you consider every day until you cross the start-line as a part of your race preparation. Think carefully about the cake, chocolate, candies and alcohol that you might be wanting and how that fits in with your vision of yourself as a **lean-mean-desert-marathon-racing-**

machine.

Some tips on eating fewer calories

If you want to be trimmer for your desert marathon and move a little faster, you may consider your weight and daily calorie intake. Here are some tips:

- **Don't eat absent-mindedly**. By this, I mean don't eat while watching television or doing something else, research shows you eat far more and don't realise you are full as when you think about it.

- Eat slowly, **put the snack down in-between mouthfuls**, step away from the pretzels. This will increase your enjoyment of food more and will enable you to get the full signal from your belly before it is painful.

- Have a **glass of water** with each meal or perhaps before you snack. It's not that your system needs vast amounts of water or that the toxins need flushing, both of which are scientifically a load of rubbish, it is simply that part of the full signal comes from gastric distension (stomach stretching). Meaning having a full belly even if it is from water will give a you a partially full feeling and you might then take in fewer actual calories.

▪ **Don't eat because you are unhappy**, this is quite a common thing to do and no matter how much you eat you aren't going to be able to compensate for what is missing. It's an understandable and perfectly normal thing to do but it isn't helpful or good for you. Comfort eating does work a little and can lift your mood for a few minutes, but puts lots of unhelpful calories in. If instead you went for a short run of twenty minutes that may well make you feel better than the snack would, the run puts a lot fewer calories in (they actually decrease) and contributes to your training.

▪ **Think of yourself as an ultra-athlete (in the making)**. You have this body which is an amazing machine and is going to power you around 250km of some of the world's most challenging terrain and conditions. You owe it to yourself to fuel it correctly. A jet fighter doesn't run too well on four-star or even super-unleaded gas, it needs high octane aviation fuel. Your body needs carbohydrates, protein, vegetables, porridge and fruit not doughnuts, fries, cake, cookies and chocolate. You don't need a diet book to tell you this. Get into the habit of every time you put a drink to your lips or a piece of food goes into your mouth asking yourself: *'is this is good fuel for an ultra-athlete who is going to the Sahara to race?'* You will probably know the answer and some intelligence used here can pay massive dividends.

Alcohol and caffeine

On the subject of alcohol I would like to draw your attention to two features of this colorless volatile liquid, firstly that it is addictive and secondly that calories contained within it aren't always useful for running.

If your alcohol intake is regular and you drink most days, there is a chance that during the race in the desert you might miss it and you might get withdrawal symptoms. It is unlikely that you fall into this group (as you are an ultra-athlete in the making), but it would be better to consider this now rather than when you sat on a square of carpet in the middle of the Sahara, feeling the urge and the shakes. It is best if you aren't quite sure, to perhaps taper down your intake a smidgen in the weeks before you set off for hot sandy climes.

The calories part of the alcohol issue is just to point out that if you are finding it a challenge to reach your target weight, then one of the easiest steps you can take to decrease your daily calorie intake is to remove the alcohol. This step alone can make a significant difference and may be all you need to do. My patients who try this, take about four to six weeks to establish this new alcohol free pattern as a habit. Then they feel that they don't really miss it after a while, as the months slip by. Many feel a lot better in themselves, with a clearer head and a sunnier deposition too.

Caffeine addiction is real. Some people experience horrible headaches for up to a week after stopping caffeine. This can come on as early as one day after stopping. If you are a coffee fiend, and you will know if you are - then have a week or two when you experiment with having none and see how it affects you. It is good to find this out in advance.

You may be lucky, I was. I regularly drink many cups of filter coffee a day and I didn't miss it at all on some experimental weeks of dropping my caffeine intake to zero. That having said, I knew that I enjoyed the caffeine sensation and chose to take a single caffeine infused gel for each day.

Using caffeine while running can give some people too much of a diuretic effect. This means they produce more urine and the bladder is irritated meaning frequent pit stops to emptyit. More alarming for many are tummy cramps and sometimes uncontrollable bowels. I do recommend you try this somewhere relatively safe before you find out what effects caffeine has on you.

If you take more than one caffeine gel or to use caffeine tablets such as *pro-plus* which are sold to the public in pharmacies and drug-stores (they are also nice and light to carry), please be aware that too much caffeine counts as a stimulant and a performance enhancing drug which is against the spirits of the competition and against the rules of international athletics under which we all agree to abide when signing up the race.

You could be randomly drug tested. If you finish in the top twenty, urine testing is the order of the day, though they could choose to take blood samples. It would be a shame to fail this test (which is required by international athletics rules), on having too much caffeine on board, by not having thought about it properly.

Performance enhancing drugs

If you are considering whether to take anabolic steroids or other performance enhancing drugs and would like my advice, then - don't. They aren't good for you and you know perfectly well that the spirit of international competition is against this. This includes autologous bloods transfusion and use of erythropoietin (collectively known as blood doping) as made popularly aware by the press following exposure of the cyclist Lance Armstrong among others.

On the edge of what is and what isn't acceptable is high altitude training. This is very expensive in terms of costs and of time. If you can afford this - do it. For the rest of us, good old fashioned normal training is all we have at our disposal to help us prepare for our world class performance attempt.

Just in case you're curious about the Moroccans who often win the MdS and similar events. There is nothing to support any genetic theory about why they might be particularly good at this. No science backs the Moroccans being better in the heat either. Anybody's heat training can match them after three months no matter where you were born or what your cultural heritage is. The adaptations achieved will be at nearly 90% of theirs within two to three weeks.

Skin colour is irrelevant too. The proposed theory of people from some nations being better adapted for running in these type of events has been disproved. There is more genetic variability within people living in these conditions than between African runners and pale runners from the rainy North of Europe.

Growing up at high altitude, running at an early age, living in a culture which lauds runners and barefoot running as a child do seem to be helpful factors for long distance success. Also helpful in growing your children to be great distance runners is coming from an area where incomes are low, as the big prize money of international races is a lure, as is the heritage of famous runners being part of one's cultural background (where they are stars to be idolized and emulated from a young age).

Training camps

Several members of my tent had attended one of the official MdS training camps in France in the months before the race. They waxed lyrical about the experience. Laurence Klein (a previous lady's MdS winner) was among the coaches. They felt that the price tag was well worth it and the experience gained, they felt to be invaluable.

Included in the great tips, tactics and information they received were two they wanted to share. The first of the two best takeaway messages were to **tighten your straps each day** on your pack. Your pack will of course become progressively lighter and less full as you merrily eat your way through the contents. As there becomes more space relative to the number of dinners remaining, the contents bounce around more. Bouncing produces an inefficient gait and is uncomfortable. So tighten those straps.

The other tip was to do very little training with a heavy pack. Instead, do runs with a light pack, but make them very fast. Doing **high intensity fast training** was argued by the international experts on the training camp to yield the best benefits to your running economy, which is of vital importance in the race. I did not do enough of this - but will do next time, if of course I'm ever lucky enough to have another go.

Sleeping on your gravel driveway

Most people take an inflatable mattress or sleeping pad with them. This is for comfort and to help fend off the cold which seeps into you by lying directly on the ground (strictly speaking, the heat seeps away by the physical property of conductance).

One of the benefits of my Raidlight bag, I discovered after I had purchased, was the built in ground mat. This is hidden behind a secret (well, it isn't now) compartment at the back of the main compartment accessed by pulling on a Velcro seam. This revealed square of white foam pad is very light but very functional. It maintains comfort of your back during the day by protecting you from your lumpy haphazard packing and by night can be placed under your bony prominences; these are your sacrum, anterior superior iliac spines and your greater trochanters if you'd like the technical terms.

Bony prominences are the lumpy bits of you what stick out. If you do not think you have any, then I recommend you take a good book, go into your kitchen and lie down on the cold hard floor (no cushions allowed). Read your book there for a couple of hours and then try and get some sleep. If you want to add a bit more realism in preparation for the levels of comfort you might expect at night during the race, you should lie on a gravel driveway - preferably near the sounds of several people slowly sawing many pieces of wood (to get the authentic snoring effect). Perhaps you could get an accomplice to occasionally kick you or elbow you in the ribs or legs. They should too bring clumps of manure and some rotting cheese to help recreate that aromatic, fermenting, tent environment.

Often at night in camp the Berbers, journalists, doctors and caterers hold fun parties and get drunk because they are all essentially on holiday. They stay up as late as ten or even two a.m. This contrasts starkly with your tent bedtime of half an hour after it gets dark, which will soon become apparent as being at about half past seven. Dawn is about six o'clock, though your bladder may have different ideas of morning-time.

Nocturnal peeing does have the advantage of encouraging a little walk - where you can see the amazing stars, though you may well each night wish you weren't quite so well hydrated. Climbing out of your sleeping bag and emerging into the chilly night can be quite bracing. With a torch you will wake everyone and increase your popularity, without the torch you risk kicking people and tents in the gloom, maybe tripping over guy ropes and possibly collapsing a tent, duly also scoring valuable popularity points.

four

Injuries and body stuff

It would be a shame to pay all of the money to enter, buy all the kit, do all of the training, only to have your race spoiled by an injury. Not all injuries are preventable. But many are.

Keeping yourself healthy goes a long way to improving your body's resilience to niggles and knocks. We are taught to work hard and to play hard. This works to a degree but you also need to train intelligently, eat well, rest well and sleep. A lot.

Does running cause arthritis?

Running prevents arthritis.

You have heard talk about getting on the bike to decrease repetitive strain on joints - I hear the coaches at my gym talking about this. But, it is not born out of very good science I'm afraid. If you feelyou are repeatedly stressing a joint identically you are probably on a treadmill and landing on your heels - get out more, that's all, and then go off road. Most aches and pains are likely to simply vanish after a few miles or a few short sessions and you will be doing your legs and body much more good.

People say runners get arthritis from all their running. This again I'm pleased to say is based on bad science. Nearly half of us are going to get arthritis at some point. A lot of people run, so a lot of runners are going to get arthritis. This doesn't mean it was the running that caused or worsened the joint pains and swellings of arthritis (Latin for *swollen joint*).

Repeated road running with high impact (either because of being overweight, bad running form or huge numbers of miles - well over eighty a week) can produce a mild increase in the knee joint wear. It is mostly counterbalanced by the increased benefits that you get to the heart, your brain, your sex life and better functioning mental health. If your biomechanics are bad (you are made wonky) or do twisting with a heavy pack like the Marines (25 kilo bergens) then you are going to increase this wear and tear.

The benefits of a trail to help distribute the forces through the knee is probably because nearly every foot fall is slightly different causing different distribution of the stresses and this actually strengthens the joints. This comes as a result of the combination of the forces around the joint. The muscles acting on and around the joint strengthen, the reflexes are sharpened and the ligaments and tendons which attach to bone in turn become stronger through repeated use.

Osteoporosis too is staved off by lots of running, which brings safety benefits in later life through fewer and milder injuries from falls, fewer falls and increased mobility into our old(er) age.

I find it amazing there are so few twisted ankles in trail runners who can run at a pace of six minute miles or faster on uneven ground, in the rain, in the dark with only a head-torch. I'm nowhere near that standard, but it is over twenty-five years since my last twisted ankle and I don't really run very cautiously. My patients who troop up to the emergency department week-in and week-out for their X-rays because they feel they must have broken their ankle and turn out only to have a sprain tend to be mainly overweight, non sporty, with a surprising number of these sprains involving high-heels and alcohol.

The moral of the story = do more, not less. If you stress your joints more vigorously and more often, they will adapt to help and support you, just the way nature intended.

Your joints evolved to carry you on your feet over varied

terrain and are specifically excellent for running for many hours. Your joints were meant to allow you to run and accordingly they don't really deteriorate because you run. Which is quite handy when thinking about preparing for your next MdS.

Though make sure you have a reasonably good technique, aren't too tubby and run off road where you can. There is sadly no evidence that running actually decreases knee arthritis. In my medical practice most of the arthritis I see is in people who are overweight, they often don't believe they are overweight as they are the same shape as many of the people in their lives and in society today, but their body mass index is over 25. This might sound harsh, but the powerful evolutionary drives which have given us these fantastic bodies weren't designed to carry the amount of lard that we do.

Because running helps burn calories, makes us fitter with a higher muscle bulk (which burns more energy) and suppresses appetite, we will carry less around the middle and thus this will preserve our joints as best we can.

Regular training sessions

Getting your training into a habit is important, as regular work towards your goal will produce a stronger fitter you. Regular training sessions spread throughout the week will give better results than if you simply use each Sunday to go at everything with great gusto and then need six days to fully recover.

I had a running coach (the excellent ex-international runner Julian Goater who I highly recommend) who said the goal of any training session is to be able to train again tomorrow. I cannot recommend this strongly enough - bear it in mind in every training session.

Adjust your session on the fly if you have to. On the way round be flexible enough so if you don't feel great, simply turn around and head for home. Give up early and live to fight another day rather than slavishly sticking to your schedule. Use body awareness to inform you when you need to decrease the intensity. This will help to keep you injury free for years.

Having rest days

Rest and recuperation are important for several reasons. Refuelling, mending of damaged tissues, remodelling of muscle fibres, improved adaptations at a cellular and a biochemical level along with vital psychological rest are a few of the many benefits.

Actually taking full rest days is easier for some people to be persuaded on than others. They are really beneficial and the proportion of actual rest days needed goes up depending how much of a senior runner you are. I used to be able to run every day, now three to four days a week of training seem about right for me in my mid forties.

If you would like to go out to train but feel rest could help, consider going for a recovery run. One which is so short or so slow that you feel more rested when you return than when you set out. These are a good opportunity to run with slower runners or simply to enjoy the scenery and the freshness of being outside (I *do* hope you are training outside).

Mending of damaged tissues is vital to maintaining your health throughout any training cycle. When you rest, you give your body a chance to repair the damage of the last training session.

Depending what you've just done, this may take anywhere from a few hours to a few days. Typically most of the repair work is complete within one or two days.

Body adaptations happen on the days you rest. Remodelling of muscle fibres and adaptation at a cellular level will occur faster and more efficiently in the first one or two days following a training session. Resting adequately to enable this to happen at the optimal rate is therefore really important. Though resting for too long can mean missed opportunities to train different parts of you. Varying what you do works best. Top level athletes have a week which includes sprints, hill sessions, strength work, rest days and a long slow distance session to build endurance.

These weekly cycles are called microcycles (in the sports science descriptors of periodisation) and a series of a few of them are referred to as mesoocycles. Macrocycles are the whole year of planning, or six months of event specific preparation. For every three weeks of higher intensity training, a lighter week can provide an opportunity for your body to perform the physiological changes needed to consolidate all your hard work. Athletes who miss out on the lighter weeks run the risk of physical and psychological burn out. They also increase the risk of picking up injuries.

Refuelling

When you run, your body needs fuel. Glycogen is the primary running fuel of your body. Your body stores glycogen mainly in the muscles and a bit in the liver. Your body can even make more glycogen on the fly, as you are going along. But not much. So if you are going to be running for longer than you have stores for, you will inevitably run out of go-go juice.

When your glycogen fuel tank runs dry you will probably either feel terrible or slow down. To prevent this unpleasant sensation or to make it go away once it has arrived, you will need adequate stores for what you are doing, or to take on board fuel as you go (or both). Drinks and food can both contain suitable fuel. Find out in training what works well for you.

Refuelling efficiently after a run involves getting carbohydrates and protein into your top end. Your body will do the rest. The best timing for this is ideally within about the first twenty minutes after a run (a chocolate milkshake or a banana will hit the spot and be about perfect, there is no need to buy expensive sports products here). But the science here isn't very well researched. This is a best current guess, so don't fret too much if you don't manage this, you will be fine.

* * *

When you train your body to run further and faster by repeated hard training sessions, your body increases the amount of glycogen stored in your muscles and liver. Which is nice. When the glycogen runs out you don't die, you merely switch over to a less efficient way of propelling yourself. This changeover feels unpleasant and you end up going a bit a slower. This is called **hitting the wall**.

When you train more, you increase the distance you run at speed before you hit the wall. When racing, if you go slow enough, or eat enough food as you go, you may be able to run without hitting this wall at all. More on this later, in the nutrition section.

Psychological rest

If you train every day you may burn out and become mentally exhausted.

Avoid this by taking breaks and vary your training. It may be enough to simply vary your training session from day to day. Rotating between hill work, fast sprints, slow recovery runs and long slow distances gives the area you have just worked on the best chance to recover, repair and adapt. Your brain will also feel better if you vary your training. It will really help your motivation for your training in general, if your brain feels it has got enough rest.

Adequate sleep is an important part of this rest. Our bodies and brains both need on average a full eight hours sleep. Our bodies do a lot of repair work to tissues at night and it helps to maintain an efficient immune system (which not only fights infections, but staves off cancer too). When we are asleep, our brains process the information they have taken in during the day. This organization is crucial for clear thinking, decreased stress levels, problem solving abilities and the efficient filing away of each days experiences into our memories.

Skip sleep at your peril. You have been warned.

Seriously though, most of us don't get enough of it, it feels good and it is *really* good for you.

Chafing

Before I got to the sands of the Sahara, I hadn't ever run in the heat. I hadn't run in my shorts with a backpack on for more than a marathon. I cannot recommend that level of forward thinking and preparation.

I mostly got away with it, though don't recommend leaving this to chance. I'm not too tubby and I'm fortunate my thighs don't rub together. As such I've never had a chafing issue with my running shorts (they are not a high fashion item. They sport a retro style: skimpy, high split sides, with a separate underpant sewn in).

In my training and in various races I experienced no shorts related problems at all. I thought my comfortable shorts would serve me well. Until that is, I got to the Sahara. In the desert sun, the sweat evaporated nicely from everywhere apart from my back, this wetness wicked down the t-shirt, into the shorts and clung sodden to the gusset. The undercarriage of my shorts and everything covering my butt were sodden. Wet through and cold. For days.

The salt that seeped from my pores thickened in heavy crusty layers by the hour. My nice smooth inner shorts turned into a scratchy white **sandpapering torture device**. This unpleasant cold piece of newly abrasive material swung, sodden every single step of the way against my upper inner thighs, slowly removing the delicate layers of skin by persistent erosion.

I don't want to labour the point, but am keen you learn from my errors. Please understand that while I love those running shorts and they were by far the lightest available, chosen because they were light to carry and were designed to give lots of nice airy breeze. They are not my recommendation for you.

You may want to wear Lycra. You may well be very pleased you did. No amount of Vaseline or body glide could protect my red raw patches, every day I struggled with this pain until eventually I gave up on any shred of public decency and used the draw string to hoist the offending fabric up out of the way. Fortune smiled on me and I've escaped the official photographs capturing the true glory of my novel shorts arrangement as I crossed the finish line. Though at the time, the pain relief was so blessed that I was beyond caring about such a trivial thing as my modesty. Plus it was a warm day.

Should you take painkillers?

The popular choice is yes. Medically that might not necessarily be the best thing to do.

Most people from the UK elect to take ibuprofen, naproxen or diclofenac as they are easily available. Ibuprofen can be bought over the counter, naproxen and diclofenac are widely prescribed by GPs. Advil and Voltarol are trade names for diclofenac.

These belong to a group of medicines known as anti-inflammatories. Specifically they are non-steroidal anti-inflammatory drugs (NSAIDs). They carry the advantages of being a powerful painkiller, having a rapid onset of action, few interactions with other medications and the bonus of anti-inflammatory actions.

These sound on the face of it, quite a good idea to be taking.

There are a few downsides though. Diclofenac has fallen out of favour as it has been shown to increase the risk of having a **heart attack** (myocardial infarction or acute coronary syndrome) about seven-fold. Even if your background risk is low, that is enough to put most people off. It isn't really much stronger than ibuprofen and if you really need something more powerful than ibuprofen then I recommend naproxen (in the UK this is a prescription only medicine - so you will have to ask your friendly GP to prescribe some for you). I chose not to take any painkillers for the reasons listed below (and of course the unnecessary weight, as every little counts).

NSAIDs cause tummy irritation and this can lead to **fatal stomach bleeds**. This is rare but becomes more likely if they are taken long term and on an empty stomach. NSAIDs can cause nausea and if you aren't used to taking them you may assume the cause of your new nausea is from something else. If you are asthmatic there is about a ten percent chance that NSAIDs will trigger an asthma attack. If you become dangerously dehydrated then your kidneys will be particularly sensitive to damage from medications, including ...Yes, you guessed it - NSAIDs. There is a chance that you could become dehydrated in this race and this is yet another one of the reasons that I did not risk taking these medicines.

When your muscles are sore this is due in part to inflammation. The reason why something becomes inflamed is because there is an active repair process going on. There is an accompanying pain signal to encourage you to adequately rest the painful body part. I appreciate the the MdS requires us to continue to race day after day and that adequate rest will have wait. These pain signals can be usefully turned down a bit to help you feel like running day after day. **Paracetamol** (acetaminophen) would be a better choice here as it has **none** of the above problems. The pain killing property has about the same power as ibuprofen and it doesn't blunt the active healing process going on in the background.

The slowing down of the natural healing inflammation process by ibuprofen is controversial, not because it isn't effective but the anti-inflammatory effect of ibuprofen is small (though cumulative). It has the lowest effect of all the NSAIDs and it needs to be taken three times a day for about a week to ramp up to its maximum effectiveness.

There is a medical condition called *rhabdomyolysis* in which hot, over used, tired, dehydrated muscles are exposed to repeated trauma (conditions not entirely unlike a desert multi-day race in Southern Morocco) - some people's muscles start to break down. This causes severe pain with cramps affecting any muscles of the body and the breakdown products start to damage the kidneys. This is potentially fatal as the kidneys can completely fail. It is made a whole lot more serious in the presence of NSAIDs. I've had it, it's not very nice, needs treating in hospital, potentially needs dialysis and on the whole is best avoided.

There is also a school of thought that taking painkillers during extreme sports might lead you to feel that you are in better shape than you really are and might not hear useful pain signals from the body. There is the risk you might not slow down or modify your technique as much as you perhaps should. In this situation you might end up damaging the affected body part more.

From a doctor perspective I'm not sure how real that effect actually is, given that the painkillers we are talking about don't blunt your sensations as much as taking something more powerful such as morphine. I felt on balance that there wasn't any need for me to take any painkiller of any variety with me. I would stick by that choice again.

In contrast, many of my tent mates and people I spoke to, felt that they were helped enormously by their various painkilling remedies and medications. I wondered if the *placebo* effect was producing most of the benefits they described to me. I chose not to mention this to any of them, as I wanted them to be as happy as possible. Also I believe strongly that the placebo effect can be used for good, accordingly if this was working well then it was certainly not my place to disabuse them (with my arrogant opinions).

The short version perhaps is to take painkillers if you think they will help you, but to also exercise some caution, bearing the notes above in mind.

Coryza (running nose)

I have discovered a new medical condition and named it running nose.

Coryza is a medical word for snotty dribbling discharge. Technically this can be used to describe both a clear discharge or a green mucopurulent nasal ooze.

I was not prepared for how much my nose would run. From my arrival in Ouarzazate to the day I left it ran. Constantly. Unlike me.

I couldn't determine if it was a dose of the common cold, hay fever (seasonal allergic rhinitis), reaction to sand up it, or what. It affected other people in the tent, so the infectious cold theory is possible. The idea that they were copying my affectation of persistent and frequent sniffing, day and night, so they could appear to others to be more like me as their hero seems less plausible.

There is good medical evidence that runners are more prone to colds after running a marathon. There was sneezing from me too to accompany the childlike sniffing-without-end. As I'm prone to hay fever in the UK I had taken antihistamines with me, though they didn't make any difference so I stopped bothering to take them after a few days and threw them into the rubbish bag (to save on weight - *every little helps*).

The sniffing was a general irritation both to me and my fellow tent mates. It was also irksome to have one's nasal passages blocked at night, as this obstruction definitely impaired a good night's sleep. The main issue and concern when you suffer from running nose was running out of tissue. My six squares of Andrex quilted goodness and single wet-wipe a day rations that I had so carefully calculated and counted (I had, after all, only done the math for toileting needs), proved a little inadequate. I hope have better luck or that you travel better prepared.

Tissue issues & medications

I hear that in the Special Boat Service they use the military standards for toilet paper ration. This is apparently four squares per man per day. Up-stroke, down-stroke, side-swipe and polisher. I elected for the luxurious six a day option and trusted that the loperamide would work in case of emergency. This was a tactic which worked well, all apart from the hugely irritating nasal drip and sniff. I carried soggy tissue like a street urchin. It was all rather unpleasant. As an upside at least the tissue dried nicely in the warming, hot breeze, though it did become a tad sandy.

I don't have a solution to these challenges from this experience, so next time I'd do the same (with more tissue). I wasn't comfortable but I got round adequately.

Apart from the antihistamines (I took four), I took loperamide (10 capsules). This is the magic medicine sold under various trade names such as Imodium which helps to slow the bowels down and stop diarrhoea. In camp the day before the race, I needed four trips to the one-man white tents.

I'm typically a one visit per day sort of chap and like some predictability with what my bowels are going to be doing. Later on I managed to get my pre-race routine carefully sorted. It was so precise that I could time this special morning visit, thirty minutes after the cold slurry which was supposed to be porridge, in what was to pass for my breakfast. This level of reliability is handy if you want to rely on not needing to go all day, as the MdS was a race setting where there aren't any handy facilities.

Used to having a routine, I was duly alarmed by four undignified episodes of rapid shuffling to the toilet cubicle just before race-day. Two loperamide later and I was back to normal. As if by magic. I cannot tell if was something eaten (unlikely), some salad rinsed in dodgy local water (possible) or contact with a virus from some contaminated surface, someone's hand or one of my patients before I left the UK (most likely of all).

I recommend packing loperamide. I hope you won't need it but you may be very grateful to have it. Being caught short when you are a long way from home would not enhance your enjoyment of the whole experience. Washing and clothes laundering facilities are a little limited. I don't need to say more.

I took alcohol hand gel with me. I obtained a tiny sample bottle from a medical rep and used this each morning after my visit and each evening upon returning to camp before eating.

Some people use a lot more but I was weight conscious and wanted to take the optimum. Some hand rinsing can be done with the spare water, but as I didn't take soap this would have yielded limited cleaning power. For next time, a tiny chunk of soap will be on my list. There is more than enough water left over after food preparation and drinking for cleaning and freshening up. This would have felt good to do periodically.

The call of nature

In my research about racing and camp life I found little that discussed the basics of life such as showers, hand washing facilities and so on. I later discovered that this was because there weren't any such facilities.

There is not much written covering the even baser functions. I will now redress the balance. But I warn you, it's not very pretty.

Having a wee in the desert consists of wandering off, having your wee and returning. You may be fairly new to performing your toilet functions in and among other people in the big bold outdoors under a beautiful blue sky. Handily you get to try this out nice and early before you even get to the desert proper. When the coaches stop by the side of the road for luncheon you will get your first chance of many.

The rules are nice and simple: **Don't trip, watch out for rocks, thorns, and think about the wind direction**. As there aren't proper bushes the ladies usually wander off in a different direction from the chaps. As the week progresses people wander progressively and conspicuously less far as inhibitions dissolve. It isn't quite the rapid descent into animalism and savagery as vividly imagined by authors such as William Golding in his '*Lord of the Flies*', but you certainly get the general idea.

Defaecating, doing a number two, aving a poop or dropping the kids off at the pool involves either wandering further, digging a hole and then covering up after you are done, or using the tent cubicles at camp. It is considered poor etiquette and seriously bad form not to dig and bury, though I can't quite remember why (other than the obvious aesthetics, slip / trip hazard and basic aroma issues). Digging is relatively easy as the ground is forgiving and there are plenty of small rocks to use (using rocks like this, squatting down on the desert floor does bring to my mind the opening scenes of '*2001 A Space Odyssey*') . If you have no handy toilet tissue, I'm told that all is not lost.

Being caught short and having no paper apparently is all about technique. Or so I am reliably informed. For your wider education here you are: The technique involves waiting until you are absolutely ready, then dropping the shorts and undies, squatting, using your hands to part your buttocks and anus as wide as they go. Emptying as required (nonchalant whistling or tuneful singing optional). Then reversing the previous moves before your legs cramp up and your knees start to complain under the strain of sitting in a position used as torture by some of the world's military regimes (known as *the stress position*).

In our race the tent cubicles were more luxurious than I had expected. They were set a small distance from the main tents, they had a flap which served as a front door and offered a significant and (for me at least - I have short legs) a total level of privacy which I hadn't really expected and was most pleased to find. They had scented wipes and flushing toilets. Ok, there were no wipes, scented or otherwise and there was certainly no flush. One took one's poop bag which was a suitably brown colored bin-liner and placed this over the sitting frame. Next you perform what needs to be performed into the center and then remove the bag. Tie up the corners and place in the trashcan outside. Berbers empty the trashcans several times a day, which must be a really shitty job.

Depending on the time of day there can be ten or so people in the queue outside, so timing is of the essence. It may prove time effective to walk further to one with a shorter queue. This is particularly true if there is one of the cubicles out of action (when someone with fewer and less morals has elected to not use a bag). The cubicles are typically grouped in threes.

While the frames are excellent, there was a certain amount of breakage that inevitably occurred with twelve hundred or so users. When descending into position for your performance, perhaps you may wish to slow your descent compared to the rate back home. If you drop down too fast and yours is a frame where only three corners are still intact, then you may topple. So a little caution here is urged. The results might not be too pretty.

If you have a lot waste material to off-load, consider a tactical wee first. This is because both solid and liquid have to fit into the bag and it would be unfortunate to fill it right up to the brim and thus have your undercarriage dangle amongst the contents. I would rather you considered this unlikely event than be wide-eyed surprised one day in April.

The last delicate points are on wiping. Point number one; please be careful with your limited supply (keep it dry in your pack and don't use it all up on day one). The second wiping point is that with a bog-standard back-at-home bowl there is plenty of room to delve. In the desert there is less delving space.

The key here is to either be very careful that the back of your delving hand doesn't accidentally become too involved with what you've just deposited or that you engage your quads and elevate yourself.

The two difficulties with the elevation method are that your quads might not be quite up to the challenge and that minor elevation here produces a narrowing of the natal cleft. The buttock space narrows and may hamper your wiping style. Just a thought.

More chafing issues

It is worth being aware that your skin is delicate over most of your body. It is after all the largest organ. There are some portions which have thickened up (the layers have more protective keratin in them) and this happens as an adaptive response to repeated mild trauma. The soles of our feet thicken up nicely when we train more, this is part of changes which can be vital in blister prevention. Preparing your feet is something that many of us pay attention to but we can neglect other areas of our skin.

The upper parts of the inside of our thighs, may for example merit the use of some Lycra. Practice with your pack and find out if your upper inside arms rub. This can be prevented by using different clothing options. Experiment with these until you find what works best for you.

In terms of lubrication there is now a wide range of products on the market. Adverts, websites and fancy packaging will try to sell you the product, so will not necessarily give you the most unbiased information on whether it will be the best one for you.

People seem to become quite passionate about their favourite lubrication (or on using none) and will tell you in great detail why their chosen method is simply the best. But what works for someone else might not work for you. What works in one situation for you, won't necessarily be the best choice every time. It is probably worth trying a few options and again, finding your best choice.

I appreciate this doesn't make it easy for you to make a decision, but I want to help you, not just tell you what works for me. Traditionally people used vaseline or talcum powder. These have largely been superseded by modern products. But they are cheap. Talc has the disadvantage that it tends to clump when wet. These clumps can then form tiny hard knobbly bits which can scrape at you like little pieces of grit. Vaseline is a pretty good, cheap preparation that will not be very well absorbed into the skin.

The problem with the expensive, nice-feeling lubrication products is they can be absorbed into the skin during several hours of use. This is a potential logistical problem as you then need to reapply the lubrication mid-race. Not only is the ground covered with sand, sometimes the air is full of it too. The lube needs to be handy - and you rapidly fill all of the available accessible slots on your pack. When you apply lubrication to your skin, it can attract tiny particles. Like sand. There will be sand. Sometimes this sand is in the air. It is a shame if the freshly applied lubrication to your tender body part then acquires a dusting of sand. As a plus point, repeated sandpapering of delicate anatomy parts can certainly take you mind off tired legs and painful toenails.

On a more detailed (and perhaps a little too detailed) note - gentlemen who have been circumcised need to pay attention to their glans penis (the knob) as when this is bounced around in sweaty undies for many hours, it can result in a really unpleasant chafing injury. Prevention is much better than a cure (applying a great gobbet of morning vaseline generally works well). As a minor consolation, if you gain one of these preventable injuries it won't cause any permanent damage. The scabs will take a couple of weeks to drop off and sadly those weeks won't be much fun for either you or your fun-partners.

Nipples are more a problem for male runners than for the ladies (the brassiere tends to protect the delicate nipple skin reasonably well). The delicate pink, fawn, or chestnut brown nipple skin not only may be chafed, but may become sunburned while enjoying the afternoon sunshine. Consider using some sunblock if you decide to expose the world to the sight of your naked chest. While running it is prudent to use **nipple plasters**. These can be any plasters (Band-aids). The stickier the better, mine lasted about three days each before the sweat and the general mooby movement caused them to fall away. If you manage to get them to stay for on the entire race they are easily removed in the post-race bath or shower.

Should one remove one's nipple hair, I hear you cry? Well, the answer is all down to personal preference but the plasters stay on better to, and are more kindly removed from, a hairless nipple (and areola - which is the colored portion around the sticky-outy nubbin bit).

The other main region to be considered for hair removal is the back. Your pack will move around, it will bounce up and down while you run and this can cause the skin to be flayed from your back. This was **a torture method in the Middle Ages**. For good reason. It is not nice.

If your back is of the more hairy variety, you will be more at risk of rubbing and soreness from your pack. What tends to happen is the hairs are repeatedly pulled, causing a painful red dotty rash of inflamed follicles as they are being yanked out. This is substantially better for those with a less rug-like back. Many runners find that applying tape to their back and shoulders helps to lessen the chafing. Having a lighter pack is probably a better solution.

Applying tape is best done by someone else and this may need to be applied, ripped off then reapplied each day. Reapplication is needed because during each day's run, the tape tends to move around, becomes partly detached and rucks up. Allowing the skin breathe periodically and dry out is important in blister prevention.

One should of course pay attention to the way items are placed within the pack. Arrange them in such a way that they don't bounce around. Tighten all the available straps and adjust them for optimal comfort. Your pack will lighten as the week progresses - items are discarded, lost, broken, jettisoned and eaten - you should tighten and readjust your straps at least daily. Mid-race tightening can provide extra comfort from the bounce.

Bouncing around is something the happens to both male nipples and the whole of the female breast. I have it on good authority that there are videos available on the internet which demonstrate this amply and in slow motion. Breast bounce is uncomfortable and whatever your size and shape it can be prevented by wearing correctly fitted, well designed gear. It is worth visiting a specialist sports bra specialist to get the optimal fit for your shape. A good sports bra can be quite expensive but worth every dime. Your aim is to run in comfort, without pain. In the last few years technology and materials have advanced in leaps and bounds and are well worth checking out in a reputable shop. In the UK, *lessbounce.co.uk* is one such shop.

Sore muscles

Muscles become sore when they are damaged. The soreness is due to chemicals released during the healing process. The pain signal is protective. It makes us want to change our behaviour so that it doesn't hurt. We do this to stop the muscle hurting, allow the sore part to rest and healing happens more quickly. This increases our chances of survival. This has been ingrained over millions of years as a survival strategy. It is a very good one. It is why pain feels so unpleasant.

The pain signal in essence gets us to stop further damage and urges us to place ourselves in the optimal situation for healing (**rest and recovery**). These signals are important and we should pay attention to them. If we were animals, we would crawl under a bush for three weeks until we either died or got better. Being human, we tend to regard pain as a nuisance and try hard to ignore it, medicate it away and generally not pay too much attention to precisely what it is and how exactly we've caused it. And they say animals are dumb.

If you tear a muscle, this, perhaps not surprisingly, hurts. Each muscle has thousands of fibers, which if over-stretched can tear. Often a muscle tear only affects a few or even a few hundred of the fibers. The torn ends bleed immediately and the blood that leaks out into the tissues is very irritant. This local chemical irritant effect is coupled with the signal from the torn and tattered ends of disrupted nerve fibers combining to given an overwhelmingly painful sensation. This makes sense, because there are lots of ragged ends your body will need to carefully knit together during a repair to make a functioning contracting motor unit once more.

If you are repeatedly and stubbornly contracting the damaged muscle, pulling these ends apart, then rapid healing is going to be impaired. So a pain signal which tells you in no uncertain terms to not move your muscle would be a great adaptive response to build into an organism by many generations of evolution. This is precisely what has happened. It may help us to learn to listen to the signals and think about how best to manage them, rather than ignore all of them. By degrees, a small tear can be ignored as the whole of the muscle will still function at virtually full strength. A big tear cannot be ignored and means your race is over. There are however some things we can do to prevent these tears.

Tear prevention:
- making the muscles stronger in the first place.
- using the muscles efficiently.
- avoiding situations where these may be stretched beyond their stretchy limit.
- best recovery.
- careful return to action after minor or major damage.

Our muscles are made up of motor units. These motor units are functional groups made from hundreds of bundles of individual muscle fibers. Each muscle can contract some or all of these motor units at a time to shorten the muscle to generate movement and / or power. The more motor units it recruits to work at the same time, the more power generated by the muscle. Doing strength training increases the number of units that can activated at any one time. The recruitment of more motor units seems to be under central (brain), though unconscious control and may be the explanation behind the superhuman phenomena where we hear of examples of people performing superhuman fears of strength in extreme situations.

Mothers are apparently sometimes able to lift cars off their trapped infants. Presumably this happens when every available motor unit is activated at once and at maximum power, with no regard to the risk of injury to self. In normal life, the recruitment is down regulated to maintain safe levels of functioning (which prevents injury), although that produces less than maximum power when racing. This is Noakes' *Central Governor Theory*.

If you would like to get more racing power, it is going to be helpful to be able to recruit more of the motor units to be active at any one time. This can be done and is best achieved by specific work with heavy weights. The two best methods to improve the explosive power of the muscles (where more motor units are active) are to work with lifting the heaviest weight you can manage and perform explosive actions. Explosive action work (*plyometrics*) includes actions such as jumping from a squat position and other similar dramatic fast exercises.

When racing long distances it can be helpful to adjust your gait from time to time. There does not need to be a massive change, but by altering how you land, your pelvic tilt or your stride length by only a centimeter or two you will engage different motor units and will cycle between them within your major muscle groups. This variation of muscle group use helps inoculate you against fatigue. You can make these fine tuning adjustments consciously, but in addition your body does a lot of this rotation between muscle groups automatically in muscles that are well trained for endurance.

Smaller amounts of muscle damage than the tears above are known as micro tears and micro trauma. This accumulated damage causes a feeling muscle soreness and this signal clearly tells you to rest. This soreness does not affect the functioning, (much) and can be safely (if not easily) ignored for a few days in a race situation such as the MdS. Sore, achy, stiff muscles is a feeling familiar to many of us.

Delayed onset muscle soreness (DOMS) is the name given to muscle pains, often severe, which arise a day or two after a bout exercise which exceeds that which you are adequately trained for. You can delay the onset by simply exercising every day it seems. You also can avoid it by being adequately trained for whatever it is that you are attempting. So when changing or increasing your training and pushing yourself, don't increase by too much too rapidly. The most common mistake it to increase the mileage run each week too rapidly.

The last important cause of muscle soreness for us to consider here is the pain of an exhausted muscle. It is important to look after your muscles after the day's exercise when you get back to camp (or at home when you are training). This, if done well, can have a big impact on your next day's performance. Looking after your muscles involves stretching, cooling, rehydrating and re-fuelling.

The technique of sitting in ice baths used by the world's elite athletes is sadly not practical out in the desert. In the desert there is no ice. The closest you will manage is applying water to soak your garments. Stand in the wind to allow them to air-dry by evaporation - this cools the garment and your muscles in it. Once this is done, take off any compression garments to allow more direct air-cooling of your muscles. Once you are cooler feel free to reapply the compression garments.

Nutrition after each race day (or after the training session - as the same principles apply):

- Early nutrition is very important here with good evidence to support to benefits of getting food into you early.
- Try to get this energy replacement food in during the first hour, if not the very first twenty minutes after you stop.
- Sugars and protein in a ratio of 4:1 seems to be ideal from the most up to date evidence.
- Handily a chocolate milk shake is about ideal.

I took this **chocolate drink** with me to the desert in the form of *Nesquik* powder and skimmed milk powder. I added a spoonful (10g precisely) of a commercial protein powder to the bag as I was trying to achieve particularly high protein content. Having tried this out for real, I feel the protein powder wasn't really required and didn't taste as nice for general recovery drink purposes, so would omit this step next time. If you add more skimmed milk powder and make it with real milk you obtain a rather pleasant malty taste, though the extra milk powder does make it much harder to get it all to dissolve. The real milk option was not open to me during the race sadly. Despite there being a cow among the competitors.

Whatever nutrition you can get into your top end during the first twenty minutes is better than nothing. Carbohydrates and proteins are ideal, making nuts and chocolate less ideal as their fat content is high. The science behind wanting early nutrition is that your muscles find it easiest to take up carbohydrate in the immediately post-active phase. This makes sense biologically, as when you run out of energy it would be sensible to get the organism to slow down a bit. Also when it does slow down it would make sense to have a biological signal which tells the organisms not to move off again until it is adequately fueled. An organism which refueled rapidly would have a survival advantage.

It seems that consuming some protein with the carbohydrates helps to stave off some of the pain from minor muscle damage. Muscles depleted of glycogen can be painful along with the pain from minor damage. The early repair of micro trauma from repeated muscular activity such as running a marathon seems to be helped if there is extra protein arriving in the gut to be absorbed. This makes sense, as you need enough basic building blocks on board to repair the muscles, which are nearly all protein in their make up.

When you are relaxing in your sandy tent, with your nice cool legs (you can sprinkle water over them and sit in the shade), with plenty of nutrition on board, then rehydrating comes next. Drink until you are no longer thirsty. Don't make things too complex. **Thirst is a useful signal. Drink until it goes away.** Thirst is a brilliantly sensitive mechanism for telling us when we are dehydrated - or not. It evolved over millennia to be as good as it is. Listen to it. It will be correct. It also saves you from thinking too hard about the technicalities of what, when and where would be best for you to take. This is helpful.

When fed and watered, the next part of your looking after your race leg muscles is stretching, massage and rollering. These are in order of actual benefit and scientific basis.

Stretching the warm muscle is important (stretching cold ones went out of fashion some twenty years ago as it was found to cause actual harm by increasing the number of injuries such as muscle tears and ligamentous sprains). Hold each stretch for thirty seconds and then relax slightly before pushing further for another thirty seconds. This is a slow process but you don't have much of an excuse as you have nothing else to do for hours before the next day's racing. This is well worth considering as part of your daily training routine too.

Massage seems to help. Softly knead the sore parts of your muscles and smooth over any tender lumps or knots by gentle massage. This has no compelling scientific basis despite being in popular and elite practice for many decades now.

There are many who use rollering at home and for some people it really seems to help. This really does have no evidence to support it - so only do it if it feels good (that is probably a good enough way to assess most things). There are companies who make a lot of money out of selling knobbly bits of plastic in the shape of a large rolling pin. Only buy one if it seems to be helpful for you.

One of my tent mates had taken a tennis ball for this purpose and was kind enough to lend it out for which we were all very grateful. There is virtually no science to support this but it seems to feel nice and that is often worth doing for that reason alone. Most things that feel nice do so because for many thousands of years of evolution they conferred some benefit to our ancestors either in terms of survival or replication. A good rule of thumb to follow for most training practices is that if it feels good then do it and if it feels bad then don't.

This is probably a better rule to follow during recovery and rest after injury than during training, as pushing yourself to the limit of what you can do is how our body best adapts for improvement. The German über-philosopher Friedrich Nietzsche famously wrote:

"Was mich nicht umbringt, macht mich stärker."
What does not kill me, makes me stronger.

* * *

This principle is present in biology - hormesis. It follows that to improve we may need to hurt a little or at least be pushed to the very edge of our comfort zones.

five

Feet

The fear of blisters scares a lot of would be runners. These raised white blebs of presumed horrific torture are shrouded in mystery, materializing from thin air to weak havoc. It is true that acquiring a blister can turn a perfectly good race into a really painful day out. Desert marathons and in particular the MdS seem to be famous for blisters. These can really hamper your race and even cause people to pull out altogether. Seven out of eight competitors from my tent visited the medics to have their blisters treated. Most of them attended daily. I'm told it was a pretty painful experience, not offset by the attractiveness of the medical crew. Mostly.

The thing about blisters is that *they are a lot more predictable than folk lore would have you believe.* A blister is a bit of fluid inbetween a skin layer. In the sports context, a blister is usually caused by rubbing. This rubbing is more likely to cause a blister if there is heat generated and if the skin is wet or moist. One piece of skin becomes lifted from the layer below it and that gap fills with serous fluid (which seeps from the underlying tissue). When you put pressure on this newly formed blister, the tension at the margins causes a tearing sensation as the fluid tries to squeeze out along the edges.

To take all the power out of the blister and to stop it hurting you should decompress it. Take the tension out by deflating it and then not put pressure on it afterwards. The delicate under layers of skin are rather sensitive as you may already know. I'm not a fan of completely deroofing blisters as I believe the upper layers of skin are protective. I believe protection of delicate, richly innervated under layers of skin is best well served by what should be there naturally; skin. The top layers of skin. I think to routinely remove this seems daft.

Deroofing blisters is the doc trotters (the medic crew on the MdS) preferred treatment method. As these doctors and medics are the ones who you have to see on the race, this may happen to you too. They do see a lot of blisters, so perhaps their strategy has some merit - though I'm not convinced it is the optimal treatment for many smaller blisters. They also use generous quantities of an iodine based antiseptic. When I'm treating my own blisters I don't bother with antiseptic, though I understand the theory of why people use it.

One of my tent mates got really badly infected blisters. I don't know if they would have been worse if iodine hadn't been used. Anyway, you are given iodine sticks to self-administer if you need to attend to your own blisters midway through a stage. These are given to you along with your salt-tablets during the check-in process and kit inspection, they form part of the compulsory emergency kit. If you need to use these, please note that they will bring tears to your eyes and a poetic song to your lips. They smart and sting a little when applied to an open wound. In theory however they will disinfect it and kill plenty of unwanted, pesky germs.

- **Heat**
- **Friction**
- **Wet**

This is the *evil triad*. The big three. Preventing blisters is about making sure the evil trio don't all appear at once. If your skin has two out of three trying to create those pesky blisters then you will probably be ok. Once you get all three then it is a tug-of-war between your skin and the evil triad. If your skin is in better condition it will last out for longer when subjected to heat, friction and wet. Eat well with plenty of protein and vitamins, this will help your skin. It will help if you have nice thick skin where it might get rubbed. If you have well fitted shoes and socks, these will help too.

When you run, your feet become hot, they sweat and they slide around your shoes. Perfect for getting blisters (which is one of the reasons that I'm sceptical about needing shoes two sizes too big). The further you run, the more times your foot hits the ground, which is why people get blisters when they run their first marathon and they run further than they've ever run before. Quite why you wouldn't want to practice running the proper marathon distance in training eludes me. If you get dirt, grit and stones in your shoes they are going to give you lots of tiny sharp edges to squash into your delicate feet with each and every step.

In the desert you will have **heat**, you will have **friction** and you will have **wet**. Desert marathons have really good blister forming conditions. You will have hot feet, you will have sand and grit in your shoes and your gaiters will contribute massively to your feet being super-duper extra humid from your sweat. A perfect state for blister formation. When your skin is permanently hot and wet, this isn't good. Wet, soggy skin becomes white, on the thickened palms and soles it wrinkles up and loses a lot of its tensile strength. Meaning it it doesn't protect you as well, becoming easily macerated.

The flesh can literally be torn away in strips to reveal the delicate stuff underneath. You might want to think about gaiters which can let water-vapour out. Parachute silk is supposed to stop air going through it (by design). They look rather stylish and can be worn up to the knees but I wonder if having sweaty feet gives them an overall negative score.

Good nutrition and running a vast number of miles each week in well fitting running shoes should mean that you hardly every get blisters (unless you are carrying too much weight). During my race I sustained one blister of two millimetres on the tip of one toe on day two. I put a hole in it with my blade and that was the end of it. No more.

The two photographs which follow are from two runners who struggled with blisters. Their packs were heavier than mine and they didn't train with so many miles. Mainly I suspect they were a bit unlucky. What was remarkable was the smiles they managed every day despite what we found in their shoes at the end. They are both amazing guys and I absolutely take my hat off to their bravery.

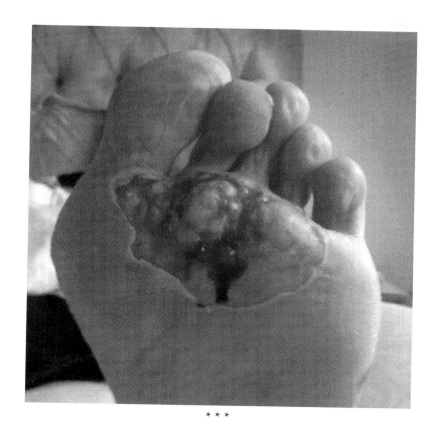

* * *

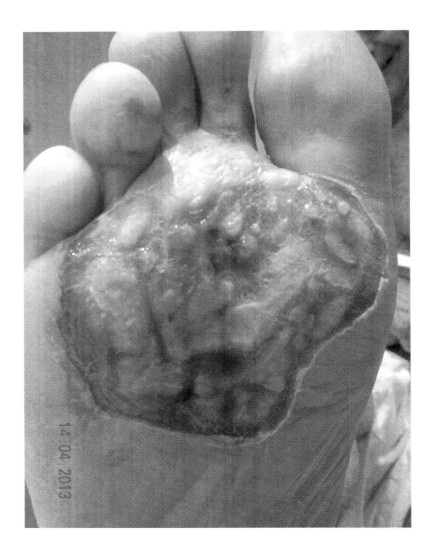

The gaiter debate

When a novice runner sees photographs of the Marathon des Sables they may be struck by the funny things the runners have on their legs. Few competitors will have used gaiters before the event or even know much about them. The have some benefits, but are not compulsory. You don't have to run in these and a few don't.

To decision to use or not to use gaiters seems have come down in favor of using gaiters many years ago. When the MdS was first run, it was run in either normal running shoes or in trekking boots. Most competitors now use a running or a trail shoe and attach gaiters to this shoe.

Which version of gaiter depends on personal preference. There are several different types and each type has a loud crowd who claim it to be the superior choice. Whenever in life there are conflicting views which all sound plausible and each point of view seems convinced they have the answer, the probable answer is that *they are all more or less as good as each other.*

The point of gaiters is that they prevent sand or very fine dust getting into your shoes or socks. The more sand you carry in your footwear, the more abrasive particles there are to cause damage such as blisters. Gaiters are lightweight pieces of material which fasten to the shoe near the sole covering of the upper part of the shoe. They then attach up around the ankle or higher up around the calf.

They are either permanent or are removable. Having the gaiter sewn or glued to the shoe permanently allows for a more secure bond and decreases the chance of gaps appearing during the race. The alternative method it to have a piece of velcro attached to the shoe running all the way around. This may be glued, sewn, or both. Velcro is also sewn on to the gaiter allowing it to be removed after the day's racing. This allows the shoe to be worn around the camp without the cumbersome, hot, sweaty gaiter.

Gaiters may be made from porous material allowing the feet to breathe (this mainly means that the sweat has a chance of evaporating) or non-porous material which is better for preventing fine sand in. There are gaiters available for general trail running which are to keep small rocks and debris out of the shoe. These can be helpful for trail runs back at home - though please note that if it is a muddy run, they can become clogged with mud and choosing no gaiter at all could be the better option. These cheap and widely available gaiters are chosen by very few competitors for the MdS as they will not keep much sand out of your shoes.

How sweaty do your feet get? Fine dust can be very abrasive when mixed with sweat in the shoe and sock. If you are a heavy sweater, you may select a more breathable gaiter.

Get a very good fit to the sole of the shoe. Allow absolutely no gaps for fine dust to pass through. Use mastic or other commercially available flexible sealant if need be. I strongly recommend sending the shoes away to a professional cobbler to have the velcro or gaiter attached. This only cost me about £25, including posting of to and from a reputable cobbler.

I posted the new shiny but ordinary looking running shoes and they reappeared ten days later, magically transformed into shoes for dessert marathons. I chose a breathable gaiter and the smallest, lightest that I could find. I removed it each afternoon. I'd go for this again.

The velcro stayed well attached to the shoe - and remains there today, still perfectly in place, collecting grass and debris during my trail runs back home. The velcro fastening for me held the gaiter firmly in place and allowed no sand up any gaps. I was able to keep my gaiter intact and thorns and rocks fortunately didn't tear me any ventilation holes. Others were not so lucky.

If you get a tear in your gaiter, this will render them useless. There are a surprisingly large number of opportunities to tear your gaiters on your desert marathon, even if you are really careful. Stumbling among rocks can undo the best of your intentions and a lot of the rocks are very sharp. Similarly, the scrubby bushes you encounter on the route can have some very sharp thorns. Some of these plants aren't even as tall as your ankle and even these can be sharp enough to pierce your gaiter.

Duct tape (plastic tape with fabric strands) seems to be the most popular and effective choice for gaiter repair back at camp. Our tent's fastest runner had parachute silk gaiters. I'm lucky that when he paused to tape a hole in his gaiters after a stiff ascent on day two I was able to pass him for my highest place finish and the only day I arrived back first. I had no idea he had stopped, honestly. A marginally hollow victory. But they all count.

Practice in your enormous shoes

There are some recommendations in chat rooms and on discussion boards about shoe sizes and running desert marathons. The general theme is that selecting your usual shoe size would be a mistake as one's feet may swell in the heat and with the damage your feet will sustain. The debate then continues as to whether one or two sizes larger is the better choice. It is probably worth bearing in mind that well fitted shoes feel nice and one or two sizes larger feel like boats and change the way you run.

Swollen feet is caused mainly by fluid which would normally circulate in your body, but for one reason or another has leaked out into the tissues. This is called oedema . Other forms of English drop the elegant diphthong and spell it edema. Different people vary with their tendency to get this. As it is fluid, this can be drained to a large extent by adequate foot elevation. This means bringing the foot and ankle higher than the heart. It takes about six hours to make a decent indent.

Practical options here are to lie on your back in the camp, head on a pillow, with your feet up on your pack. Although you will lie down at night, most people wriggle off any elevation while they sleep and then your feet will be at the same level as your heart. This is not nearly as efficient. Fluid flows downhill. Please don't wait until night time to get your feet up if you have oedema.

Oedema is worse if you are low on body protein. It is worse if you have poor nutrition. It is worse if you get your salt balance wrong. It is worse if your kidneys aren't working well. The other cause of foot swelling is inflammation (hot, red and tender). There is little you can do about this as it takes days to go away.

My opinion is biased. I am in a lucky minority. My feet don't swell in the heat. They barely swell after some very long races. I managed to notice a tiny bit of swelling after a hundred miles, just enough to leave a sock mark. So I didn't need shoes of any different size. Many of my tent mates used shoes of one extra size. One of them got a fair bit of impressive looking foot swelling so he was grateful for the bigger shoes and the others were generally pleased with their over sized shoes. They found the accumulated layers of taping applied by doc trotters to their blisters made their feet up to the size of the roomy shoes.

There were various sock strategies. Some people liked a fresh pair each day and would rotate two pairs. While one pair was worn, the other air dried on the pack. I think this might make them rather sandy, but no one complained of this. I used one pair for the week which simply became progressively aromatic and smellier as the week wore on. I found that worked well for my ten pinkies and I knew that having worn them a lot in training that I would know how my feet would feel. I knew my feet wouldn't swell much so I was comfortable with this choice. My sock choice was a lightweight *Injinji* sock. These have five little pockets - one for each of your toes. They worked well with my foot shape and I didn't blister. Putting them on was a faff, but I had a cunning strategy to make it easier.

* * *

I took with me a small chunk of a stick deodorant. I didn't take the whole stick as I was being ridiculously obsessive about weight. Cutting down every gram I could think of. This was of course a bit silly because I was overweight and not a fast enough runner for it to make much of a meaningful difference, but there you go.

I reasoned that my feet sweat and the less sweat they produce, the less soggy the skin will become and the less prone to blister formation. I went on to reason that if an antiperspirant worked on my under arm regions (axillae) to keep them drier, then the same product should work on my feet. There are tips on internet forums and in books about using foot lubricants to help ease chafing in socks for ultra distance racing. When I have tried these, the lubricant simply made the sock a bit soggy and didn't have a noticeable difference to blister formation. I did notice a lighter wallet.

Using the antiperspirant deodorant on my feet gave me the optimal blend of lightly lubricated feet and less sweating. I'm not sure if it achieved the aim, but fitting the toe-socks on feet that were slightly slippery was helpful. Unwrapping it from its cling-film cover, my small square of magic to grease my foot certainly looked a unique preparation. This square inevitably crumbled into a bit of a mess as the week wore on, but I was able to use it each day.

Some people used a double sock method and they swore by this as the best technique. This involves using, you guessed it, two pairs of socks. Again, whichever you think might work well for you, please try it out in practice sessions. over and over again. It is best not to get any surprises from your kit.

Foot preparations

Your feet will get fewer blisters if you have tougher skin. The skin will harden in response to natural stresses. This is good thing and one way the body is naturally well adapted to walk and run long distances. If you have a high mileage to your walking or your running, then the number of times an hour your feet hit the ground will be very high.

Every time your foot lands, it slides around a tiny amount when it makes contact with the ground and the shoes around it, via the sock. This ends up with the skin in all the chafing places developing and thickening by the laying down of extra keratin in the cells. Practically speaking, this means the skin thickens and hardens in all the right places. This will stand you in very good stead for the race and comes highly recommended.

All skin can undergo this adaptive response. Guitar players find that their skin changes with practice. The left hand has to hold the string against the fretboard to make a clean sound. When they start playing, the fingertips are often very tender after every practice session and in some cases, may even bleed. As guitar players play more, the fingertip skin hardens. This also happens to the skin on the feet of regular runners. The process by which the skin thickens is known as *keratinisation*.

Keratin is the waterproofing and protecting agent in the skin. The skin cells contain more or less keratin depending on how that body part is being used. Some regions of the skin are better at adapting to this than others. The palms and soles are the best at adapting, though every area can do it to a smaller degree.

When hardening the skin on your feet for running, you might think the harder it is the better. There is a limit though and if the skin layers are thickening too, then the skin can become brittle and painfully split. You are aiming for the soft supple feel of a very expensive pair of leather gloves. This thickening of the skin can happen if your have an inflammatory process in your skin (such as dermatitis) or if you have pitted keratolysis (a smelly infection giving you moth eaten looking skin on your soles - if you get this, see a doctor and ask to have your *Corynebacterium* eradicated).

Generally, if you run a lot of miles each week (perhaps about forty) then within a month or two, your foot skin will have become thicker and remain supple. It is skin like this which is best resistant to blister formation. This thick feeling skin, like fine soft leather, is the reward for the long hours running and the pay-off for the efforts you have made in getting yourself out of the door (even on the days that your didn't fancy it as much).

It is possible to harden the feet artificially through using white spirit, surgical spirit or commercially available products specifically for foot hardening. I chose to use a product which is used on greyhounds to help them out with their naturally soft paw pads. This seems effective, makes a mess and smells fairly pungent (much to my wife's dismay), I used *Tuf-foot*, so cannot comment about other brands. It does produce a yellow stain of the skin after application.

* * *

Safety note - absolutely do not use white spirit and smoke at the same time (be well clear of any other flammable products too). On a general point - *don't smoke at all* - this will make your race harder. I did spot a couple of competitors smoking while around the camp in the evenings. I'm not sure whether to be impressed. I found it all quite tricky enough with my lungs working at their full capacity.

I'm not a fan of taping my feet, because I've not had great success with that. A lot of people find it very helpful, I would recommend a lot of practice and learning of the skill of taping if you are going to do it. You can use fabric tape of various brands, such as 3M, applying this tape before you race to weak spots you regularly encounter. I know of many competitors who taped their feet in advance of each stage. An advantage of taping is that there is a fabric layer which can take some of the brunt out of chafing and thus protect the skin underneath.

It is important not try anything new during the race. You should be very used to whatever it is that you do. When you are tired and not thinking after a stage or in the morning before the next, you could do without learning a new technical skill like taping.

When I've used taping, the tape came off. It ended up as a soggy mess and made the run more uncomfortable. Where the tape partially came away, the ends rucked and bunched up in my sock. On one occasion where my feet became wet, the removal of the tape also took away the skin to which the tape was attached. All of it.

six

Kit

Different desert marathons have differing kit lists. The Marathon des Sables is a 250km foot race in the Sahara. Each competitor is expected to be self-sufficient through the race. This means carrying your safety gear, your food, your sleeping gear and your own medical supplies. You are expected to carry sufficient water to last you safely until the next check point. This section is based around the MdS compulsory kit list, but the general principles can be applied to any ultra-marathon distance race.

Choosing the kit you will take with you and the food you will take is part of the whole challenge. Most of us thoroughly enjoyed the planning. Here follow a few tips about things I got right. But a lot of stuff I got wrong too.

Safety stuff

Safety is important. The desert is a dangerous place. If things go wrong, they can go wrong very quickly. The compulsory kit is all about your personal safety.

The MdS is a race across one hundred and fifty miles of desert with over a thousand competitors. The potential for things to go wrong is high. Don't panic. If you are sensible and follow the rules and instructions you will be ok. In terms of real risk, I find it helpful to consider that the MdS is a fantastically well organized commercial event that cannot afford bad publicity through serious injury, death or loss of competitors.

Consequently the ratio of staff to competitor is very high. Your progress is constantly electronically monitored from check point to check point and if you don't arrive when you are predicted to by your times, someone will come looking for you in pretty much the place where you could have got to. Safety features include vehicles, helicopters and access to fixed wing planes. They even now have full GPS tracking.

You are also pretty unlikely to become lost. Even if you are wandering along like a Muppet in full numpty mode.

All the check points have to be set up and thus accessed by vehicle. Mostly there are tracks leading off into the distance from the start line and they lead to the next check point. Where there are dunes there are compass bearings which I can testify are pretty idiot proof. There are multiple two foot square signs with direction arrows along the route every mile or so. These are painted with fluorescent paint and very easy to spot and follow.

The compulsory kit is supposed to mean that you can survive if things take a turn for the worst. I saw lots of flares let off during my race. Many people clearly felt at the time they had an emergency, so used their flares - perhaps a little over-excitedly with the benefit of hindsight. Though it is reassuring to know that if you set off a flare, that within minutes a rescue vehicle or helicopter will come and collect you.

Food is a compulsory item. The race is a self-sufficiency race. You are expected to carry enough food with you for each day. Carrying 2000 calories per day is the minimum. This is checked at the beginning during race registration and may be checked randomly at any point after. I don't know of anyone who finished outside the top twenty having an extra food check. These amounts are sensible minimums and it is part of the race rules to adhere to them. Carrying liquids or powders doesn't count towards these totals. Only solid food counts. Energy gels do count.

Stuff you have to buy and take along with you on the compulsory list:

- Backpack - you have to take one of these. Carrying all of your stuff in your hands wouldn't be practical. You have to take a pack to carry your gear. There are various different designs. Take the lightest you can find which suits you. Twenty liters should be sufficient capacity. Avoid an internal frame (they are heavy). Most have external strings - these are useful towards the end of the week when you have less contents and this can tighten the pack down - which decreases bounce as you run (thus decreasing chafing and is considerably less annoying). My pack was a *Raidlight* with two water bottles and a front pack - this bounced. A lot. I cannot recommend a front pack if you plan to do some running.

▪   Sleeping bag - it gets cold at night. When you are tired and running low on energy, you are more susceptible to hypothermia. Yes really. Even in the desert.

▪   Head torch with spare batteries - the torch is vital for running after dark and we will all be running in the dark on the long day. Having spare batteries is sensible. Carrying spares is routine in ultra-endurance events as part of the mandatory kit list.

▪   10 safety pins - You have a running number on the front and on the back. This uses eight pins. Two are spares. I took flimsy lightweight pins and was surprised when they became bent out of shape during the week. Take adequate pins (number and girth).

▪   Compass with a one to two degree precision - having a compass to follow is sensible and it needs to be sufficiently accurate. Some compasses have glow in the dark numbers. I don't feel they are a necessary feature as when you are using it you will have your head torch. If your head torch has stopped working you should probably either make camp for the night, light a fire or set off a flare.

- Lighter - this is a sensible precaution in case you become lost. You can ignite vegetation to start a fire. This will generate smoke for people to find you or to keep you warm at night. Keeping warm is an important issue because if you find yourself lost you won't have the comfort of your bivouac. Matches could become damp and not light properly.

- A whistle - if you need to call for help, a whistle provides a noise which carries very well over long distances. This takes much less breath and energy than shouting. This is a standard safety item. Many people find a whistle inbuilt into the buckle of their chest strap on their racing packs. These are acceptable by the MdS rules, but aren't as loud as even cheap lightweight whistles.

- Knife with metal blade - this is in the compulsory kit to make cutting clothing and flesh easier in the case of an emergency. It can be used to prepare small animals and bats for eating. It can be used to fashion sticks and vegetation for survival purposes. I mainly used mine to clean my toenails along with fashioning water bottles into nice soup and cereal bowls.

- Tropical disinfectant - this I think is a typing error and should read topical. Topical means on the surface. Using alcohol cleaning skin wipes or antiseptic cream should both be adequate. Disinfecting wounds with these is only going to help a bit. If you sustain a wound, the healing will be more impaired by retained debris than infection. Wash out the wound. Use copious quantities of water if you can spare it. *The solution to pollution is dilution*. Next, clean the skin edges. Wound infections very rarely magically arise from the air, they mostly come from the patient's own bacteria which live on the skin and these will be present at the wound edges.

- Anti-venom pump - this is to cure you from snake, scorpion and spider bites. I don't know how effective they are, but perhaps even twenty per cent less venom would be nice if you are unfortunate enough to be bitten by something poisonous.

- A signaling mirror - this can be as small as only a few millimeters across and still do the job effectively. Acrylic craft mirrors are very lightweight. My compass came with a mirror, so that was an easy decision for me.

- One aluminum survival sheet - this is to keep heat in. This sheet if you use it, does not have magic powers. It will only reflect body heat which is being lost by radiation. This means that if you are already cold, it a bit late. If you aren't sure if to use it, then put it on. Ideally put it under another item such as a jacket. Wrap it around your legs. Tuck in the edges like a duvet on a cold night. Then listen to soothing sound of the rustles as you shiver.

- One tube of sun cream - becoming sunburned can be a significant but entirely preventable problem for competitors with fair skin. This means there is a single rule for everyone about carrying suncream, regardless of the skin color you are born with.

- 200 Euros or equivalent in foreign currency - this money is compulsory so if you become lost, you are able to use public transport to find your way back to civilization. You will be able to purchase food without having to rely on generosity of the public or on the event organizers. When assistance and lending of cash has been given in the past, often the lost competitor forgets to pay this back once they are safely home. Hence the rule about always carrying adequate cash. And your passport. The passport isn't on the list, but is compulsory. If you are airlifted to safety you may need to be repatriated. If your heart is still beating, you will require a passport on your person.

There are compulsory items to be carried that you don't have to purchase yourself. They will be given to you at race registration at the camp, the day before the race in exchange for handing in your luggage. The organizers provide a road-book with maps and compass bearings, a distress flare, a huge bag of salt tablets (these are coated and don't taste nasty), toilet bags (these are coated and do), plus your race numbers. You are expected to have these items with you at all times on the course. There are time penalties or disqualification for competitors found not to have the above with them.

The compulsory kit list omits to mention the electronic tag - to be worn at all times when on the course. This was a timing chip (not a GPS device) and was strapped around the ankle with a piece of velcro. I was worried about mine falling off and secured the velcro fastening with a safety pin as part of my morning race preparations. During my joyous run into each check point I heard the reassuring beep of the timing mat. Hearing this and the sounds of others around me as it registered our transponders became part of the race experience. It is now a GPS transponder - very modern and enables your family, friends, the CIA, IRS and your stalkers from back home to keep tabs on you.

The flare bounces

The flare is heavy, it also bounces around. It weighs about 375g. It bears some thinking about where in your pack it is going to go. Many competitors have theirs easy to access in case of emergency. I think that if you are letting off a flare you're probably not running and probably have time to take your pack off. I think you can put it somewhere where it doesn't bounce and isn't generally going to get in your way.

When you are hot and tired, you may be surprised to learn that simple things can become quite irritating. Perhaps this is just my grumpy disposition, certainly a lot of people seemed to have a relentless perma-smile throughout the entire event.

The strings on the pack held my flare on nicely, as there was a small pouch I could tuck the base into. Some packs don't have this handy pouch and I don't think I'd have trusted the string to hold it on its own without sliding. Not only is it potentially dangerous to lose your flare, it is littering and as it is a piece of compulsory equipment there is a hefty fine (and time penalty) for not having yours.

Technical clothing

Years ago, when the MdS was in its infancy, when Rory Coleman was new to the game, there weren't the modern fabrics we currently have to choose from. Wicking material and compression garments are now mainstream. And for good reasons.

When a piece of material is wet at one end and dry at the other, moisture seeps from the wet to the dry end. The mechanism of this is capillary action. This is the movement of water molecules between the fibers drawn along by surface tension of the fluid. Some materials are better than this than others. The propensity to do this is known as wicking.

A lot of clothing manufacturers claim these wicking properties are vital for modern sports competitors. The theory runs that when you sweat, some parts of you sweat more heavily than other parts, if your clothing can distribute that sweat effectively, this evaporates more efficiently and allows better cooling. Usually when you run, one of the limiting factors in your speed is effective heat dissipation. You will basically run better when a little cooler. Having clothing which makes this a bit better, the theory goes, should allow you to run faster.

* * *

I don't know how important wicking properties in kit are in reality. I do not know if the high price tag that some garments carry are worth it. Modern lightweight materials do seem to be better than cotton. They certainly feel nice.

I was taken in by the advertising. All the gear I wear has these claims, so I can only tell you that I got on well and think I would have been uncomfortable in cotton. I was pretty comfortable throughout my race and I think I can credit some of that to the technical impressiveness of the kit. My front and arms were always dry. My back was moist. But at the base of my back it was sodden and this extended down onto my shorts which were sodden too, especially the gusset. Not only was it sodden, but it was very cold.

That, I can assure you, felt very strange. Running along in the desert in the scorching sun, with a cold wet bottom and under crackers.

There are many runners who use compression clothing. They feel the clothes make them run faster. The theory is that muscles wobble less and therefore are in a better position for the next contraction and they thus fatigue less quickly. The users claim they *really do* feel less fatigue and that they *really do* recover faster (after all, this is what the adverts tell us). While the kit feels nice I am a little skeptical on their claims of improved muscle efficiency and decreased fatigue. They may have a point, I'm not sure I'm a good enough athlete for it to make a discernible difference. That having said, when you do the MdS you may feel that every little bit of help that you can gain from your kit is worth it.

The next time I go, I will use compression shorts. I chose not to because I thought they would be too hot. My shorts chafed horribly and the next time I will take my compression ones. I'm not sure about a compression top. There were three in our tent with these and they were all very pleased with their choices.

I saw a presentation from the *x-bionic* rep at an MdS expo and he sounded quite convincing but I thought they looked too warm for me. I do wear their socks and their winter top and these are excellent. But for the main outfit I remain unsure.

Two of my tent mates wore the outfit and swore blind that it was superb. Maybe next time I'll consider this. The theory is this knitted garment provides compression at the right places and allows moisture to efficiently wick away better than their competitor's offerings. The claim is that despite wearing a thick knitted garment which covers a lot of skin area, that this magically will keep you warm in the cold and cold in the warm. The very high price tag put me off. And they looked a little odd.

Pack weight

Once you've selected your pack, go for a short run (empty). Did you enjoy that? Then load it up with suitable weights - I recommend about 10 kilos and then go for the same run. Did you enjoy that quite as much?

After this reality check don't panic - it gets better. You may wish to train to run with a heavy pack. If you do, then start with low weights - perhaps about a kilogram. I tried to increase mine by about 1 kg a week and eventually managed some runs with 8kg and 750ml of water. In case your science classes were a while ago, one liter of water weighs one kilogram.

For the race I was going to try and get down to the minimum pack weight and was only taking a 750ml bottle. The minimum pack weight for the MdS is 6.5kg without water, but including the mandatory equipment (including the flare and so on). Many of my fellow countrymen had packs which weighed in at a magnificent 10-12 kg (and more) before their water and then filled two 750ml bottles.

If you are going to run around the desert with 13.5kg on your back you may consider some training while carrying this load.

Some schools of thought say you should train a little over your race weight. This translates as about fifteen kilograms in your pack. I know many people who don't train with a heavy pack. You may choose not to. That of course is absolutely fine, but if you would like a realistic preview then load your pack up.

Learning how the pack moves and indeed, how you move can be helpful. You may choose to wear different clothing options. You may choose to take less weight. You may decide that some taping of the skin of the shoulders is warranted. Many people are surprised at how much chafing occurs over the lower back region.

Your pace on the MdS might be a little less than you are used to at home. For example, over twenty miles of undulating trails I could run eight minute miles before I left. That took about a thousand miles of training. My ten mile road time was sixty six minutes. On the MdS I carried just over seven kilos which lightened every day by 800g - I managed about eleven minute miles at best. My fastest day was at 12 minute miles, my long day was at 18'15 pace and overall I managed 14'30 minutes per mile. I had really pushed myself too. I'm not showing off or trying to impress you (either with my speed or my slowness), merely so you've got some kind of mental benchmark.

I couldn't make my pack much lighter next time but I could have been a better runner. I could have carried less belly fat. I could have been better trained too. I would have practiced a lot more on hills, done more with uneven footwork, I would travel more often to my local beach (Bournemouth), I would lift lots more weights, do lots more initial speed work, adding in hill walking with a much heavier pack. Perhaps around 12kg. If, if, if.

The difficulties around training are many. Fitting all of this into your life, or fitting your life into training is tricky. It would no doubt have been considerably easier had I just won the lottery, didn't have to go to work, was able to motivate myself better and didn't enjoy calorie laden snacks quite as much as I do. But, hey-ho. That's life.

Increasing my pack weight over October and November of the preceding year, I ran with my full pack in training a few days each week from about December to the beginning of March. I averaged around fifty miles a week. I topped out at one 100 mile week plus a mock-up week where used annual leave to replicate the distances of the MdS. I wanted to see if I could manage the miles, day after day, with a pack (26, 26, rest day, 52, 26). I tried these big miles while eating only race snacks (jelly babies for me), plus cold expedition meals (to see if I could survive without taking a stove).

I learned that I could survive and that I didn't even need to use the posh expensive food - cold porridge and noodles were cheaper and easier to prepare whilst being even lighter.

I was fortunate to be able to have my mock-up week. Even the weather was kind and dumped six inches of snow to make the going a little more fluffy underfoot. This snow was unusual for my part of the UK, where persistent rain is the Winter norm. As with most of my pre-race preparation, the low temperatures (daytime about 4 degrees and -3 in the dark) meant that I needed running tights, several top layers, gloves, buff and a wooly hat.

I weighed myself before and after each run that week, with body fat compositions to calculate fat loss, water loss (I measured every milliliter of water that week) and energy expenditure. I analyzed the percentage composition of my food and calculated the grams eaten of the main constituents (protein, carbohydrate and fat).

I'm not recommending this level of silly obsession. It is quite unnecessary. I used this level of detail to help inform my decisions about what to take and how I thought it and I would perform. You can simply take my word for it if you'd like. I feel that I'd make even better decisions next time. These would be informed by the additional information from how it actually performed and what really happened to it all in the Sahara (once the sand gets everywhere and mentally the wheels start to fall off).

Initially I used my usual back pack to train - my 3 liter racing *Camel-bak*, this was an error because the fully laden bag pulled the chest straps right off the shoulder straps. While one can run with the belly strap on and the chest strap open - I found this changed my technique. I ended up pulling my shoulders forwards to stabilize my pack which produced some very painful pectoral muscles.

With the new pack it was better - I bought the *Raidlight* 20+4. I made the choice rather unscientifically as this was what I thought to be the popular choice, working on the assumption that other people knew more about this sort of thing than I. I'd seen lots of photos of other people doing the MdS with this pack and the only detail I knew was that it sounded impressively light on the *Raidlight* website.

I trained for hundred of miles with weights in this pack and there was minimal wear and tear. This is perhaps helpful as you won't be wanting to buy a fresh pack for the race (unless of course you've just won the lottery in which case I'm jealous).

For training weights to use in the pack, I tried a few things such as food, clothes and dumbbells. Of these, the weights were the most stupid, they bounced around and sank to the bottom of the pack despite my (what I thought at the time was ingenious) use of lots and lots of bubble wrap. Each and every time I tried to run with them they proceeded to flay the flesh from the base of my back.

Learning rather too slowly from my errors I moved to a different tactic of placing a large sleeping bag at the bottom of the pack and adding increasing number of bags of dishwasher salt. Dishwasher salt had the benefits of being readily available in my local village shop, being cheap, being in soft bags, easily bound into heavy duty dustbin (trashcan) liners and once they leaked (inevitable I'm afraid), was easily rinsed off. This salt washed out easily on a 40 degree standard wash. This splendid cycle with a standard washing powder washes the stink out of every other item of sports clothes or running shoes that I own.

Water bottles

Do you take ones with right angled pipes for squirting in the mouth? Do you take a bladder? (not the one you were born with, that one is going along for the ride anyway but a flexible water container which sits in your pack).

Packs with an inbuilt bladder such as a *Camel-bak* hold a disadvantage. They can split and spring a leak. This is inconvenient while you are training as you gain a soggy bottom. And you run out of water.

In the Sahara, it is more inconvenient to run out of water. While the checkpoints are frequent enough that you are not likely to die, this is still not ideal. The only strategy for carrying water in the race would be to then hold the 1.5l water bottles in your hand or within your pack. These are heavy and cumbersome. For these reasons, most people take water bottles. Most people have a pair of water bottles attached to the shoulder straps of their packs. A frequent choice is to fill one with water and the other with a sugary electrolyte solution.

I elected to remove one of the water bottles which arrived with my pack as I wanted to cut down on unnecessary weight. I tried this out in training and it worked for me. I found the balance wasn't an issue as I had feared. Mine was a 750ml bottle with a vertical straw and pull valve. This worked well for me. I only used water during the race, so had no need for the extra bottle.

Headlights

You are required to take a headlight. These will enable you to go for a pee at night, find your way in the dark portion of the long day and read your bedtime stories. Staff will be able to find you if you stray from the course on the long stage. The route was well marked and there wasn't too much to trip over apart from undulating sand, black rocks and tussocks of wiry grass. We were all given glow stick to tie to our packs. I didn't manage to tie mine particularly well. I found that the glow sticks are a challenge to stick to your pack and have a tendency to bounce around.

You may like to consider taking a small piece of ribbon for the express purpose for glow-stick securing (silk should come in at less than one gram and will be robust enough for the job).

Headlights are more helpful if they are brighter. What helps you to find a fuse box under the stairs may not provide much help in rolling sand dunes. Predictably I took with me Petzl's super lightweight *e-Lite*. This weighed 25 grams and was about as powerful as a glow worm with a hangover.

I considered the weight of the torch and its luminosity against the hours of battery life needed. The light will be needed most evenings in the tent and a lower light setting is kind to your tenties. Some torches have a red setting. This is helpful for night time pee journeys and is even kinder to those around you.

At home I train with a *Silva sprint plus* which is about as powerful as a car head beam on its 2.5h setting but is about 150g plus 350g for the battery pack. For the MdS you also need spare batteries. Don't forget that batteries lose their capacitance charge faster in hot (very hot) conditions. Currently the best bang for buck on the market for me is the Silva Trail II which weighs about 75g and is one of the more powerful lights for about £70. The batteries are AAA and last around twenty hours. Best value one notch up is currently the splendid Petzl Nao II. If you can afford it, buy it.

Finding your way in the night section of the long day is relatively easy as there are over a thousand of you. The slow steady march of bobbing lights is very welcome sight. You know you are on the right track and the bright lights of the camp are visible from many miles away, calling you home. The glow sticks help too. It is very easy and almost essential to buddy up.

I was pretty unwell during my last five hours and a kindly soul hobbled slowly with me and put up with my incessant grouching for about four hours. We crossed the line in a jubilant slow motion shuffle. I don't recall his name but if you read this, I am forever grateful and owe you some beers.

Poles

How do you decide to use or not to use? How European do you feel? - ultra runners in the UK and US tend not to, everyone else tends to. Presumably the inability the speak English makes your ankles weak, I really don't know.

They are available as either screw type or pull cord type. The purpose of using poles is they takes the weight off shoulders and legs. They provide stability at times. When selecting a design, I think there is a need for sand baskets. It is also a good idea to have caps on the points to prevent stabbing others in tent areas. Most of the packs on the market, including the one which you you get the hard sell on (the 'official' MdS pack from *WAA*) have pockets of straps for poles, as carrying them is too difficult. I thought that the extra weight wasn't worth the benefits for my running style.

Wearing larger shoe sizes?

You may have read or heard advice about wearing larger shoe sizes. Some peoples feet seem to swell - but not everybody's. Some people find that they are able to run fifty miles with a pack without a noticeable change in foot size.

This is why we train - to find this sort of thing out.

If you get blisters on the actual MdS then you may need to visit the doctor (Doc Trotters) for bandaging. They love their taping - they put a lot on. This will need to fit in your shoes along with your socks (are you going to wear one or two pairs?) along with your feet which may or may not have swollen significantly.

I was the only member of our tent who didn't visit the doc for taping. This is approximately representative of the non-elite runners. Seven casualties and one smug bloke. It stands as a testament to the generous kind spirit of my tent mates, that they didn't lynch me for being smug. I now of course realize that it was probably simply good fortune rather than my genetic make-up as some kind of ultra-running demigod.

I thought I prepared my feet well and therefore chose to only wear a single layer of sock - many wear two pairs. My single sock was an *Injinji* toe sock, original thickness. I selected a single layer as this was what I'd trained in and I had already found them very wearable for thirty five mile racing (though this was in the UK winter and not sand or heat). What I hadn't prepared for was kicking rocks. I kicked a lot of rocks.

I'd read an account of one elite runner who complained that he kicked rocks when he was tired. That is, he stumbled into them. I don't think when he got tired he elected to take up the sport of rock kicking like a bored child kicking a can down the street in the gutter. Something I've noticed you don't see so much nowadays.

I thought the man a simpleton - how can one fail to pick up your feet adequately to not kick rocks? What an idiot injury.

Predictably - I was the stupid one. My weak, tired little legs fatigued by blistering extreme heat meant I shoved my poor toes onto numerous small black rocks (and some large ones).

I even invented some new swear words. My advice? - accept the rock kicking, it's probably going to happen.

What this translates into is extreme toe pain every time you place your feet on the ground. This is quite a lot of times, twice a meter, 250km, this is about half a million footfalls. The pain is sometimes due to blood accumulating under the nail (black nails - *subungual haematomata*) and possibly small fractures of the ends of the toes.

I think I finished the race with two toe fractures of what was probably the distal phalanx terminal tufts. This estimate is based on my prior stupid kicking injuries. I've previously played field hockey as a goalkeeper and wasn't much good at that either -

acquiring a few broken toes due to my poor kicking technique. *Plus ça change.*

The buff and other hats

A buff is widely regarded to be a vital piece of kit.

This cheap item only weighs a few grams, can be purchased in a variety of colors, or jingoistically covered in your national flag.

A tube of material, many people wore this around their neck so that it could be easily pulled up over the face in case a sandstorm blew up. I've even seen some people with eye holes cut out, so they are wearing a desert balaclava.

Mine was included as a freebie in a goody bag after a local marathon in the UK. I could even see through it a little when it was pulled right up over the face, which certainly kept the sand out, so I didn't have to cut any eye holes. We were lucky during my MdS year and encountered no sandstorms during the day's races. Mine lived around the top of my water bottle as I found it too restrictive and too warm on my neck or wrist. This was transferred before each checkpoint so I could fill the bottle more easily, facilitating quick passage.

I found little use in the end for my buff apart from a useful snot rag after my vomiting episodes - many other people used theirs a lot more. A lot of racers wore the buff as a hat. The most popular style seemed to be the '*pirate*'. Some racers had the tail hanging down to protect their neck, some supplementing this with a peaked baseball style cap. My contribution to the growing lore of uses for your versatile buff, is as a pillow. I stuffed my down jacket and various other clothing items into it until it was a comfy looking tube.

In the UK for the six freezing months of my training it was a fantastic scarf and kept my neck nice and warm. Take one, but don't feel you have to wear it - it is quite sufficient to have it reasonably to hand on your pack somewhere.

I didn't know how my pale skin would hold up in the heat - so elected to take a cap with a built in neck flap. I chose the lightest I could find (the *Mamut* Nubian) and had to get mine sent from Germany as UK availability was limited (google translated the foreign language website more than adequately, which was handy as I am no polyglot). Sourcing scantily available items is easy over the internet if you are prepared to translate the pages written in languages that you don't speak. I can recommend this if you get stuck finding gear that you'd like, as it worked for me.

It arrived on time, was splendid and did the job perfectly. I was the only wearer of this version among the 1000 as far as I could tell. Despite being able to wear this season's brand new release after all my efforts, I was disappointed not to look very trendy. No fashionista am I. Most people still took the ever-popular *Raidlight* cap. I had the most hat envy for the very flash and light looking *Salomon* new offering, also released only a month before the race and old hat now. All these hats are pretty light, so you can take anything you like the look of as they will all do a pretty good job.

A drawback with ordering items online is you get no idea of how well they will fit. Mine had an elasticated drawstring and this proved very useful in the strong winds. The desert wind seemed to decide often that it was hat stealing time. These pesky winds tried very hard to remove my hat on many occasions with unpredictable squally gusts. The race is quite hard enough already without having to chase a hat off into the desert. Particularly if you are traversing a high ridge at the time.

Do you take sand goggles?

The answer depends on how weight conscious you are going to be. There is no doubt that sand in the eyes is unpleasant. When a sandstorm blows you will screw your eyes up against this onslaught. Tight shut against billions of tiny scratchy eroded rock particles. You should note that the sand gets everywhere. Yes, everywhere. Yes, there too.

The goggles I saw people wear were apparently comfortable and did the job well. Military issue goggles were good and effective but not as lightweight as the *Sun-dog* brand. I took none and simply used my sunglasses which were a pair of Oakley wraparounds. These proved a good choice. They were comfortable, light and robust. Neither did they bounce when I ran. You should definitely take a pair of comfortable sunnies as it is pretty bright out there in the middle of the day.

Some people used a buff pulled up over the face. This gave reasonably good protection from the sand in the eyes but I found it was uncomfortable to breathe and rapidly became fairly soggy from the moisture in the exhaled air.

Sunscreen

If you only listen to one piece of advice, trust me on the sunscreen, as Mary Schmich advises. I too urge you to wear sunscreen. I used about half a 100ml bottle of *Riemann* P20 (SPF50) spray. I'd never used this before, disliked the smell and thought it was excessively heavy.

It was despite my reticence, fantastic. Using factor fifty I had no sunburn at all. This is from a pasty pale white man fresh out of the Winter dark of the UK. Applied just the once each morning with no additional applications during the somewhat sweaty day, it was fabulous.

The single 100ml bottle was easily enough to cover my legs, arms and all exposed flesh for all of the days I was away. I wore short shorts, short gaiters and a short sleeved t-shirt, so had a lot more flesh on display to the world and the sun than many others. It is worth thinking about how much pale flesh you are going to have to cover and for how many days. The race itself, plus charity day, plus two days either side in camp and then eventually back at the hotel where you have the option of lying adjacent to a splendid pool - you aren't allowed in as we all look like moth bitten zombies at that point.

* * *

Deciding which factor sun cream will depend on a few things. Do you want a tan or do you simply want to be sure you won't burn? For me the burning issue was more important than any other.

Do you take cream or oil? I don't really know much about these things and purchased the first bottle in the *Amazon* listing.

Spray or not? I wanted to take a bottle rather than one with a spray attachment (to save a few grams on weight) but couldn't find a bottle where I looked on the internet. Although it wasn't my initial choice, I discovered that despite the extra couple of grams, I found the spray quite useful. I also only used half a bottle, so would empty half the contents before I went if I get the opportunity to have another go (fingers crossed).

Because I was nervous about getting sunburn I had several sun-bed sessions before I left so that I could get a little protection. Please note that the degree of browning gives some false reassurance as to actually how much UV protection you gain and you are still at risk of sunburn. As there was there is at least a little benefit, I gave it a try. I wouldn't say it was worth the effort, cost or the time.

I took along zinc oxide war paint for my nose, cheeks, tips of ears and lips. It worked, in as much as my nose and cheeks didn't get sunburn, but I looked ridiculous. Every time I touched my face it smeared and was probably not even needed as the factor fifty sunscreen was so effective. I would not take this next time.

Next time I would take a small sunblock lip balm and keep it handy. You drink often and it will need reapplying frequently.

Contact lenses

I'm rather short sighted with a -5 diopter prescription and thus needed to take with me either glasses or contact lenses. Without my glasses I can't really see my hand in front of my face. I hate running in glasses, as they tend to slide down my sweaty nose, so chose lenses.

Mine are the disposable type you put in and discard seven days later after a single night out of them. They've served me well for years. I was worried they might get sand in, or I might damage them rubbing my eyes.

I found they didn't accumulate too much sand and pleasingly they remained comfortable throughout the week. I had lots of sandy gloopy gunge in my eyes each morning, but a wipe with a handy piece of clothing proved sufficient to restore me to my usual beautiful self. I didn't take with me any solutions, no saline, no pots for storage. I didn't even take my spectacles to save on the weight. I took a single pair of lenses to change into half way through the race-week at the seven day point.

It was a risky strategy to change lenses during the race week and I was apprehensive. In the end it just about worked out ok, other than the actual lens changing moment. The tent was windy and dusty and my little signal mirror was woefully inadequate as a means of viewing the eye in question. I had hobbled towards a medical tent (triage was empty at seven in the morning) and asked if I could shelter out of the wind to change my lenses. They kindly agreed. The tent was dismantled by the Berbers only minutes later, so I recommend going early to do this.

Flannel

Will you take an extensive wash kit? I took no washing materials with me and found this acceptable but a little grimy. One of the limitations of this was that my daily application of sunscreen attracted dust and sand. Each day I was caked. These layers accumulated as the week wore on. I'm not sure how much a daily bird bath would have achieved.

My Retired Navy Seal room-mate took 1/4 of a flannel to freshen up at the end of each day and start the next. He declared this does not require a large amount of fresh water and the flannel quarter dries easily.

My tent comprising a marine, a professional tennis coach, two doctors, a lawyer, an investment banker along with successful entrepreneurs and a classics scholar. Three of the eight washed regularly. Two had proper shaves along the lines of British Officers in the trenches of WW1. I'm not sure how much they appreciated the olfactory delight the rest of us provided in not presenting a uniform strategy.

If you decide to take clean-up kit along with you, there seemed to be plenty of spare water each day from your allotted rations.

All of us cleaned our teeth. I may have been the only one to saw the handle of the already lightweight travel toothbrush off. I was certainly the only one to decant the toothpaste into a piece of cling film to save on weight. This, I cannot recommend. The cling film and toothpaste simply squished and smeared as it was compressed in my pack. The wrapping and rewrapping of this minty white goo was not as elegant and precise as it had seemed in my imagination beforehand. When I told my wife, she simply shook her head pityingly and left the room.

Being so careful about the weight, I took the minimum of everything and toothpaste was down to about 2ml. However it soon became clear that I didn't take quite enough toothpaste and had to eke out my tiny smears each day. This was due in part to my forgetting that while the race was only a few days, you are away from your suitcase for several more days. Before and afterwards there are days in camp. I hadn't built those days into my very finely balanced calculations.

The sawn off lightweight travel brush was excellent though and the cut-down stubby little handle wasn't an issue. Next time I'll take a children's one as I could save another 2g - but I didn't think of this.

Packing

How many days can you survive without the creature comforts that we are all used to? This not very complex calculation of days also needs to be applied to toilet paper. I hadn't thought this out adequately.

I took what I'd worked out for me to be the right number of squares (try this at home first!), four to six per day seems to be a minimum. Most normal people simply take a roll. I tried the armed forces regulation issue of four squares per man per day. I'd counted every single square and perhaps this was a little too detailed. This clearly hadn't taken into account the excessively runny guts that affected me the day before the start. Oops.

Don't forget to put your counted squares or huge toilet tissue roll into a waterproof ziplock bag, it might not rain much but your back will sweat and several parts of my pack's contents were soggy when unpacked each day. It would be sad to have your week's paper ration turn into a small piece of modern art *papiér mâché* to amuse your tent-mates with, in a guess-what-this-is competition.

A top tip is to place your sleeping bag and any clothes you

might want to wear in the afternoon away from the part of your pack most at risk of dampness. You could take along a plastic carrier bag with this very purpose in mind.

A top tip if you forget the top tip above, is to tie the soggy items to the top portion of your tent to dry in the wind and the sun upon your return. Unpack nice and early to check for damp soggy contents even if every fiber of your body wants to lie curled up in a little ball of pain gently whimpering. If you forget, don't get around to, or otherwise don't achieve this, then you may like to know that when you climb, wearily limbed into your sleeping bag at night, your body heat will tend to dry out whatever goes in there with you.

I didn't take a stove. The stoves are pretty light and the fuel too. I decided that a few days without hot food wouldn't kill me and I even tried this out in training. I wouldn't take a stove next time either. My tent mates had the opposite view and they would take one next time.

Do you take a solar charger? Can you cope without your smart phone? Can you live without music for a few days? This is worth considering as you may then need a solar charger for your device or devices.

A policy of MdS is not to disturb others and to share in the peace of the desert. There are now holidays offering the experience of NO electronic devices (they are all forbidden items) and the MdS includes this opportunity at no extra charge. My main consideration on solar chargers was the additional weight. Having said all of this, I know several people who took along lightweight chargers who seemed pretty pleased with the results they had.

Cow suit

Lots of people spend a very long time obsessing about kit details and I'm genuinely unsure if it is worth all the effort beyond making sure that you are comfortable. However ...

The year that I ran the MdS there was a Japanese competitor who ran the race dressed in a cow suit. A furry suit. A giant comedy head and a matching tail. I cannot even begin to imagine how hot he must have been. When my friend approached to ask what the reason was behind his unconventional outfit, he was expecting it to hear that it was in aid of a local children's hospital or similar. This is not the answer the chap gave. He simply said '*I like cows*'.

* * *

seven

Eating

Choosing what food to take with you for your desert marathon is all part of the fun. Some races provide food, which will probably sound rather tempting when you consider the options if your race does not. Some races are self sufficient. For the MdS you are self sufficient from the morning you wake up on race day until you cross the finish line on the last. The luxury of packed lunches and wine will have to wait. Teas and coffees? You have to brew your own. If you want a beer, then you will have to carry it.

Waist management

When you run your desert marathon you can expect your hard efforts will burn through something in the order of four or five thousand calories a day. You can expect to lose some weight during this event. Because you will be eating around two to three thousand calories a day it is worth giving the science of weight loss a little attention.

Let's start with the basics. You will not lose a dangerous amount of weight. In fact you might not even notice the loss. Many of us carry far more around our middle than we are even aware of. Fat is very high in energy and if you convert his energy for running, you can go for miles and miles. Literally.

Fat contains 3500 calories for every pound.

Let's consider a skinny male athlete who has about 8% body fat and a weight of about 136 pounds. This equates to seventeen pounds of fat in this elite runner. This means he has about sixty thousand calories stored around his body as fat. This translates into about thirty days of a five thousand calorie burn. Then MdS is only five days long. The skinny guys have plenty of spare calories stored.

For the larger runner there is even more stored energy to spare. If we think about a runner with twenty per cent body fat who weighs two hundred pounds. This chap or chapess will have enough spare around his or her middle for 140,000 calories, which would be enough for 28 days of desert running. Burning your fat for energy is only part of the picture. Most of us have lots of spare. If it was this easy then …but it isn't quite that simple.

When you lose body weight there are three big components to this:

- Fat loss.
- Water loss.
- Water released from glycogen.

Fat is converted to energy (*this is good*). There is usually an equal amount of protein loss - this comes from your muscles which then are thinner and less powerful (*this is bad*). There is water loss, which is temporary loss due to you exercising and blowing off the water in your sweat, breath and fueling the basic process of generating muscle movement. There is also the water that is bound to glycogen. For every gram of stored glycogen (think gasoline in the tank, but for muscles) there are two grams of stored water. This will be released for use to keep you a little bit better hydrated during your race day as you burn the glycogen and will need to be replenished each evening in time for the next day's efforts.

The glycogen stores in your muscles hold about enough energy to power you on a flat road for about an hour and a half. The liver then releases its supply and will take you for another half an hour. Intense training and clever carbohydrate loading will stretch this out by another half an hour. This means that most runners run out of go-go juice at about the eighteen to twenty mile mark. That, my friend is **hitting the wall**.

Training for endurance will soften this blow. If you move your athletes body efficiently, that can help, as will fueling on the hoof to help offset this situation of running on empty. When you run out of muscle and liver glycogen you switch to burning fats. Nice.

When you run out of energy in a race you don't however automatically switch to burning this energy-rich fuel. This is a little unfortunate, but you know it to be true. If it were true then anyone carrying a few extra pounds could simply run some big distances and simply burn off their belly in a few days. This doesn't happen. While it is true that running is one of the very best ways to support weight loss and to exercise fat control, like a lot of biological science and human body in particular, things are a little more complex in the real world.

When we run out of fuel, what has happened is the glycogen store in your muscles and liver have been exhausted. For every molecule of glycogen burned, two water molecules are released. This is handy because this water helps stave of dehydration. It is important to know because when it comes time to rehydrate and refuel during and after the race, that this is where some of the water is going to disappear to. I don't remember needing to go for a pee much in the afternoons. Or the evenings. My kidneys typically took until 03h00 to wake up properly. Which was nice.

Your body will burn some fat next, but it will also burn protein. This protein will come from your muscle.

Your body will actually break down some of your muscle bulk in order to propel you forwards. This seems to be a bit of a design fault and we can do a little to make this less of a real effect. It is important to pay attention to the protein because if you don't, then you will have smaller muscles as the race progresses. Smaller muscles mean less efficiency, slower running and more time out in the hot sun. This slowing down is great if you want to get the best value for money out of the race, but it is inconvenient if you want to perform to your maximum.

Taking on food supplies during and after each stage is really important to keep your muscles working as well as they can. If you are out on the course for more than about four hours you may benefit from taking on board something which contains protein. This will also help you to run faster.

There is supporting science that our bodies sense protein in the stomach and are able to free up more power for your muscles (this adds support to the *central governor theory* which is gaining ground in sports science).

After you have finished it is important to get glucose in to your system along with protein. A ratio of 4:1 carbohydrate to protein is currently in vogue. Your daily protein intake should probably be as high as you can manage. You should be aiming for two grams of protein for every kilogram of your body weight while training or racing.

Front pack and in-race fuelling

The merit of having a front pack is you can get at stuff while you are racing. Such as your venom pump. This is a good thing. The disadvantages of a front pack is that it tends to bounce a lot. For a walker I suppose this is fine as it doesn't move too much at walking pace. While running at even my slow speeds I found the perpetual up and down movement intensely irritating. Furthermore, the stretchy bungee cord I used to secure it better was inadequate and the repeated bouncing caused this to fray after thirty or so miles of my cold-weather training.

The only way I could stop my pack bounce was to use three layers of bungee wrapped around strategic portions of the pack and clip this onto my chest band. The disadvantage of attaching this to the chest band is the the placement of the race number became an issue.

The organizers are very keen on your race numbers being placed precisely and exactly as they determine and woe betide you if yours isn't visible to their satisfaction. I think this because the press and photographers make money out of selling competitors photographs and use these numbers for identification. They will claim it is because of safety and I'm sure they are right.

Removing the front pack meant the rest of the pack ended up moving around even more than before which I also found to be irksome. It seems that I was easily goaded and doomed to my fate. This probably means I was stressed and worried about something completely different and blaming it all on the pack - which was a perfectly good pack and I should have perhaps whinged a lot less that I did.

I would purchase a pack without the waist band next time around. I would consider a waist-pack or a back-pack with decent front and side pockets that I can get into without reaching around. Taking the pack off during each day's racing for me wasn't a welcome option. This is time consuming and it is supposed to be a race after all.

Given what I chose to stow in my front pack, if I hadn't taken it I would have needed to find an alternative way to access my jelly babies, my iPod with headphones, my single gel, my compass and I needed somewhere to put my trash. These could probably all be done with a pack with decent sized pockets on the waist strap.

Carrying a compressed empty water bottle (and trash you accumulate such as candy bar wrappers) merits some consideration. You might like to practice this on your training runs (or not, most people do after all just turn up and wing-it hoping for the best). You may even have two empties (1.5l plastic water bottles) at some points and whilst they are light enough to carry in your hands it is more pleasant to tuck them away.

Where you choose to tuck them can be important as your only place to dispose of them on the course is at the checkpoints and having them ready for disposal can save you valuable seconds (if of course that matters to you). If your empty bottles are in your hands, you are then able to place them easily into the wide topped bins which reside immediately behind each checkpoint as you pass through and onto the next section of the course.

Saving seconds might not seem vitally important but they do all add up. You could think instead in terms of it making you seem like you ran half a minute-per-mile better than all those who were apparently racing at the same speed but didn't get their checkpoint routine quite as slick as yours.

There is a powerful psychological boost from passing through a checkpoint in the manner of a streamlined F1 racing team at a pit-stop and seeing all the people static and relaxing as you power on through onto the course. An alternative view is that the checkpoints are a nice break and people do rest and chat there a while. These are some of the very rare shady spots in the desert.

One solitary gel per stage was my daily goo allowance. This I saved for the last third of the race each day. I elected to treat myself with a *Clif-shot* espresso flavor for a daily caffeine hit.

Next time I don't think I'd bother, I was surprised that generally I didn't really crave the creature comforts or the variety in flavors. People warned me that I might, but I'm not too surprised that monotony wasn't an issue. I was clearly conditioned. I'd unknowingly put in a lot of training at university. As a student I ate dull repetitive cold food for years and desert marathons, for all of their other challenges, mostly last less than a week.

My in-race fueling strategy was *jelly babies*. These were about perfect. They are sold in small packets with about enough for six an hour for about six hours (thirty six or so of the squidgy little figures lightly dusted with sugar. These provided sugar and virtually nothing else, are pleasantly flavored, don't stick to each other even in the heat and at 190g for 640 cals provide a good ratio of fuel for weight.

Fuel that provides a better yield of calories for weight than this means things which have a higher fat content. I'm not convinced that fuels containing a high proportion of fat are broken down quickly enough mid-race to give you most of the fuel and this then runs the risk of you becoming hypoglycaemic (low blood sugar).

Hypoglycaemia is the state known to many ultra-runners (and you are about to become an ultra-runner if you aren't already) as **bonking**. Bonking feels bad. This is the state where your circulating blood doesn't have quite enough available fuel to fuel your current activities.

The brain senses this and makes you feel awful so you want to lie down (to stop using up the limited fuel). Your vision blurs, you feel confused, your legs become sluggish, you shake, sweat and feel faint. This response is hard wired into all of us as it carries survival benefits. The advantage to the body of the horrible feeling is that you are compelled to stop moving. If you stop moving, you are then able to use more of the remaining sugar in the bloodstream to fuel the brain. If your brain runs out completely, you then fall into a coma and die. Fueling the brain is the number one priority.

While you are busy trying to race, these hypoglycaemic episodes are clearly inconvenient and you should plan well to avoid this. The fuel your leg muscles use to run you around the course is stored as glycogen. Replenishing this glycogen store is done before the race by overnight fueling. Your blood sugar is maintained by also using your liver stores. Both of these stores are enough for about two hours of racing. Anything longer than two hours and you will be needing to take on board fuel on the way round.

Eating while running or walking might not be something you've tried. The sheer practicalities of trying to eat while running form part of the challenge. Selecting the right food forms another. Having food your body can digest on the go is important.

Many find their body can only process some foods. If your body doesn't process something well, it can object. When your body objects,you get nausea, actual vomiting, tummy cramps, sweats and even diarrhoea. As all of us differ, try a range of options in training to find out which work well for you and your body.

Some people choose electrolyte drinks with glucose, some use gels, some use energy bars. Some people swear by real food and use trail mix, nuts and dried fruit. Peanut *M&M*'s are popular but I found the rattling too irritating. Jelly babies were the choice for me, although I was tempted by Kendall mint cake.

I decided powders weren't my thing as they are too fiddly to put in the water bottles at each checkpoint and didn't seem to be any lighter. Not to mention having to pass through customs with several kilos of small bags of powder, individually wrapped and labeled by hand.

I found that gels make your fingers sticky and generate sticky rubbish. I was choosing to take virtually no grams of fat with me so this ruled out anything with nuts in. Whichever of the mid-race fueling options you choose, test and try it on really long runs (also long walks). You should carry your water with you for these to get practice with managing the water too. Rehearse actually carrying a couple of liters with you and coordinate the eating and drinking.

* * *

One of my major considerations while training was my frozen little fingers. Numb with cold, I struggled with zips and pullers on the pack. I also found that in removing the gloves to gain better coordination, my fingers became so cooled during jelly baby retrieval that it took a couple more minutes to get my glove back on. I'm very pleased to be able say that in the heat of the Sahara that particular problem wasn't an issue!

With your food, there is the consideration of when to eat it. My advice is to eat early. If you eat anything with sugar in it, or indeed any more complex carbohydrates, then your body will try and control the rise in blood sugar which occurs by releasing insulin. If you are trying to run at the same time with this insulin surge, the result is that it can rapidly cause a drop in your blood sugar and produce the unpleasant symptoms of hypoglycaemia.

Having too high a blood sugar is not good for you either, which is precisely why the pancreas is designed to secrete insulin to control the level. The condition of diabetes is where your body doesn't produce enough insulin or the insulin that it does produce isn't effective (the receptors aren't receptive enough).

If possible, you may consider avoiding carbohydrates for the two to three hours before a race if it is going to be long one. Having said that, it doesn't make a huge difference, so if you don't have a choice, then eat and don't worry about it. Personally, I try to time it well. Let your your pre-race breakfast settle in your stomach, well before the start. Start your in-race fueling plan on the start line with small amounts of your chosen race fuel, then and about every fifteen to twenty minutes throughout the race.

The science behind eating early during actual racing is that the rate of absorption of fuel from your digestive tract happens at a steady rate (assuming you're not going flat out - which you probably won't be). If you absorb fuel at a steady rate, then it is a good idea to give your digestive tract a steady amount to absorb.

Eating small amounts of sugary foods or drinks makes you run faster. There is good experimental evidence to show that having glucose in your mouth every fifteen to twenty minutes gives a measurable temporary boost in performance. The actual studies were performed on cyclists in the laboratory with glucose containing and non-glucose containing liquids but these findings are felt to be appropriate to extrapolate to other endurance sports and to solid foods. I agree with this and think the reason behind the boost in performance is from increased contraction of the muscles triggered by the brain and central nervous system in response to the glucose detected in the mouth and upper pharynx (the posh word for throat).

My solution here was to eat two jelly babies every twenty minutes. In the UK when I race I eat two every two miles according to my *Suunto* GPS watch. I didn't take a GPS device with me on the actual race. In the desert I was running more slowly and a small normal watch was adequate to assist my timings here. I chose to eat every twenty minutes rather than per number of miles. This worked fairly well for me. Next time I would taking on lots more nutrition during the race.

In my tent, between the eight of us, I felt that all food solutions were represented and most of the tent were pretty happy with their choices - so feel free to take whatever seems to work best for you. Some people even stopped during race stages to cook up a meal. On their stove - with a small fire and everything. Though mainly you saw this on the long stage.

After each race-day in the tent (I mean bivouac) the most jealousy seemed to be over pork scratchings (which have a surprisingly good calorie to weight ratio) and honey roasted cashews. As someone observed, it was possible to do most of the shopping the night before the MdS in the pub and take along entirely bar-snacks.

One of my tent mates brought a selection of food which looked suspiciously like he had thought of packing some food only the night before. The selection was pretty much like he was out for a pre-race-pint and then thought; "*gosh, I really should buy some food to take with me*", and then fueled by beer and optimism had simply gone berserk with bar snacks.

He had nuts, all varieties, he had *Pepperamis*, he had a wide selection of chocolate bars accompanied by scampi fries, pork scratchings and a selection of expensive looking crisps too. I'm a little disappointed he didn't bring a pickled egg. Presumably that got eaten on the way home. We did abruptly stop the Micky taking when he very gentlemanly offered his extremely tempting bar-snacks around.

The most popular choice in terms of pleasure and mid-race performance boost was the *Pepperamis*. I have reservations on the validity of a high fat and high protein snack being physiologically capable of providing instant energy but my tent mates definitely felt a perceived significant performance boost for them. I'm not an elite, so who am I to argue.

I mention these points to illustrate that whatever my theories are, despite having a good medical science background and my believing them to be well founded, you should look at them as only a guide and if you find something better then please use that. *But trust me on the eating regularly and early.*

My food day

My day started with porridge at sunrise, which I allowed to settle in my belly for nearly three hours. The jelly babies started on the start line - though not too early as we could be standing there for half an hour or more. When the Happy Birthday's were done, with Highway to Hell blaring out of the speakers and the thundering of the helicopters passing low overhead, that was a good hint we were actually about to be underway. Two jelly babies popped in my mouth and off we go.

With one third of the race to go, each day I had my coffee gel. I'm not sure if it counts but at the finish line each day we were given a hot sweet cup of Sultan tea. It wasn't quite a cold beer, but it was very welcome nonetheless. After the finish-line, on arriving in the tent I had my chocolate shake before nibbling on my biltong. Supper consisted of two packets of super-noodles (low fat, chicken and herb flavour).

The noodles were the low fat option because I reasoned (*erroneously*) that if I took no fat with me and I ran with a calorie deficit each day then my body would either take this spare energy from my muscle bulk (I'm certainly by no means bulky) or my body fat stores. I was quite keen for the fat stores to be used if possible. If I had no fat in the diet I thought my body would be more likely to take it from the stored fat. It was a nice idea, but not sadly based on sound science. The human body is a complex piece of biological kit with the interplay between all the systems being much more complex than we frequently give it credit for. Having an adequate protein intake and using the muscles turns out to be much more important in terms of preserving muscle bulk during weight loss than dietary fat content.

Despite what I thought of as decent training, I started with a body fat percentage of fourteen per cent. This was higher than I wanted. I reasoned that I could have dropped to five to eight percentage points before any slight loss of performance and probably a lot of performance might have been gained by weighing less and thus having less weight to carry. This equated to being able to lose two pounds of fat a day safely.

Each pound of fat contains 3500 calories. I could safely have a 7000 deficit each day. I was eating 2500 each day and my estimates were that I would be expending about 3000 a day on the run on top of my daily 2000 normal requirement (basal metabolic rate). By my sums I was aiming for a loss of about 2500 calories daily. I was aiming to get a daily intake of protein sufficient to ensure this deficit was taken from my belly excess cuddle layer.

Knowing it was important to keep an adequate level of protein intake to minimise or stop any muscle breakdown, I aimed for a very high protein intake. Choosing 2g per kg of body weight each day of protein, which was at the time around the 2x 62 mark and 130g of protein each day went into the food rations.

Among the thwartings of this cunning plan was that when they fed us in the hotel, on the plane, on the coach and at the camp before the race I ate like an **oinker**! I apparently have virtually *no* willpower.

* * *

On top of this, whenever any of my chums wanted to offload some of their excess bag weight by passing on snacks, I hoovered them up. Again, like an oinker.

My returning weight and body mass was identical to when I left. This was down to the multiple meals consumed in the hotel and on the long journey home. Calorie insult was added to calorific injury when I was filled with more alcohol than I'd had in two years. So much for the vision of returning home triumphant, a trim leaner version of my former self. Thanks to the amazing sunblock I didn't even have an impressive tan. Oh well. The race wasn't really all about getting into shape and looking fitter. Still, it would have been nice.

I had very detailed plans which may have worked pretty well, if I hadn't been quite such a piggy wiggy. I would most definitely try a little (or a lot) better restraint and self control next time. In terms of food choices I would take the same, though skip the coffee gel. I might take more calories, perhaps as cashew nuts for the flavor and extra energy. I wouldn't worry about the fat content of the food next time. Maybe for me 3000 calories per day would have been better. I really hope I get to find out.

Gourmet dining choices

The recovery shake I decided on was my version of the rather unpleasant tasting commercial mixes. I believe that the sciencey sounding electrolytes and minerals that are put in these drinks have no proper scientific proof and are simply gimmicks to blind the public. The constituents I think are important are protein, carbohydrate and flavor.

I placed 38g of skimmed milk powder and 50g of *Nesquik* chocolate milk shake plus 10g of chocolate protein shake powder into a ziplock bag. I emptied these baggies of chocolatey goodness into an empty water bottle using my race number rolled into a funnel. Add about 500ml of water and you have an easy-to-drink yummy chocolate milk shake. The *Nesquik* was lovely and chocolatey, the milk powder a little malty and the unpleasant protein shake powder was well disguised. I bagged up one of these for each day.

Every day I had a food pack with the day's food in it. Upon retiring each night I poured the porridge oats into an empty water bottle using the race number funnel. This already had the skimmed milk powder mixed in. I added the water and allowed it to stand overnight. As it was in a capped bottle, it was safe from bugs and spiders. It was also ready to eat first thing as I poked my bleary eyes out of my sleeping bag. Simply use the knife to slice open the bottle and use the only other tool, the titanium spoon to eat. Discard the empty into the rubbish bag and lick the spoon clean. No washing up. Job done.

One potential disadvantage of eating the food cold was the length of time for food to rehydrate and I wanted to get the carbs into my belly as long before the start line as I could. The start times each day were at either 08h30 or 09h00 and I managed my breakfast at about six or just after. So the timing worked well for me - but only by preparing the porridge the night before. Cold porridge, *nom nom, yum yum.*

Upon my return to the camp each day I knew the importance of getting the carbohydrates into my system, along with a little protein, as soon as was practical.

I got back to the tent most days at about half past two and would decant my noodles into a water bottle as soon as I was done with my chocolate drink and biltong. These went into the sun with the lid on, to stand in the water, plus the herb sachet to cook in the sunshine (a bit). These were comfortably edible forty minutes later, though I suspect they could have been eaten sooner. In cold water in the UK they were almost ready within about an hour. Slicing the top half off the bottles to make a handy bowl was rather satisfying and a good use of the compulsory knife. I also carved the ziplock bags into shapes to facilitate easy pouring.

In case you are unfamiliar, biltong is meat which is dry cured. It can be made from a variety of meats. I chose beef which had been rolled in spices and allowed to dry in the sun. This is apparently traditional in South Africa. I took a 50g sachet for each day. I thought this is the way they eat meat from somewhere very hot, so presumably it doesn't go off in hot sunny conditions. Mine was vacuum packed too, which gave me a little extra reassurance. It tasted excellent and I would choose this again.

I took fresh biltong with me from a gourmet supplier (meaning they had a website, charged a lot and used fancy packaging), it dried out a little and wasn't as soft by the time I ate it as when it had arrived by courier, but each daily 50g pack of goodness was edible and showed no evidence of spoiling in the heat. I would recommend this. The only issue here was the toothpicks I'd packed (I even packed two so that I had a spare if one went missing) - both went missing.

When packing initially I was disappointed to discover that my kit didn't fit into my pack. This was particularly dismaying as I had been feeling rather too smug about taking less kit than anyone else I knew. I felt too that I was being Spartan with my decision to take so few obvious extra luxuries.

My solution was to take a rolling pin to the noodles and crush them. If you opt for the same solution, they need a lot more crushing than you might think before they go into the bottle. If you pour them into a decapitated bottle this is easier but you don't then feel as comfortable wandering off to leave your slowly sautéing supper as you start to worry about it blowing over or being eaten by flies. It seems that in the Sahara there are quite a lot of flies which buzz around you nearly constantly, they are quite small and love to just come and sit on your exposed bare flesh or your supper.

I deliberately chose not to take anything with curry, hot spices or chilli with me as it turns out that my bowels are apparently quite sensitive to these ingredients. I discovered this during my week long experimentation with dehydrated meals of various flavors. I discovered these choices are best avoided. I needed to be able to race with the confidence that my digestive system was going to process each day's intake.

eight

Hydration and salt

We were given a lot of salt tablets and a lot of fluid. The advice is to take it all. I chose not to take it all. This may have been an error.

Heat training

Preparing for the heat is very helpful. There a few different approaches.

You can spend time in a hot country. This would be ideal. It takes several weeks to build up 95% of your heat adaption and it takes about three weeks to lose most of it. It takes about three months to reach 100% of your acclimatisation. There is some debate about what precisely acclimation and acclimatisation actually are.

The short version is that no one can quite agree, so consider the two terms interchangeable. They are trying to describe stuff that happens to and in your body when it goes into hot places. After being there a while, everything is a bit more efficient. Just like high altitude training. A week long sunny holiday three months before you go will be nice, but confer no heat adaptation advantages on race day. When you arrive in Morocco it will be about three days before the first race day. This allows for a large amount of acclimatisation and on its own may be enough.

I had limited options for heat exposure before I went. I tried three sauna sessions a week for the preceding month. I monitored my heart rate, complete with watch and sexy looking chest strap. I took a room thermometer and a tympanic (ear) thermometer in with me. The thermometers were for my trying to measure my change in body temperature before and after the sauna and then the cooling swim. I was reluctant to use an anal probe to get an accurate core body temperature reading, it was a public gym after all. The change in temperatures recorded could act as a proxy measurement when combined with the heart rate to estimate change in core temperature, which were more practicable than a precise reading.

The room temp went up higher than my gadget, so this stopped working with a blank screen. The ear thermometer didn't work as my ears had sweat in them and this water had gained heat, rendering the infra-red reading of my tympanic membrane (ear drum) inaccurate. The heart rate monitor told me that by sitting in in a sauna to the point at which I felt very uncomfortable, my heart rate went from seventy to about one hundred and forty in the intervening twenty minutes. I was so unfit that swimming to cool down to a comfortable temperature simply kept my heart rate at about 140 before returning to the sauna and there my heart rate stayed.

I have no idea if these shenanigans were actually of any benefit. It felt quite nice and made me feel like I was doing something useful before I went. Given that I was otherwise sitting on my tushy thinking I was tapering, I should have probably done some gentle runs, or strength work, or any other number of things. It's amazing what you can justify to yourself.

Commercial companies have heat chambers which they will charge you large sums of money to run in. The idea is that you run in these with a pack on while they monitor various of your physiological parameters (such as heart rate, VO2 max, speed, core temperature - probably just tympanic and so on). While I think these could be useful in terms of learning what it will feel like on the MdS, they aren't usually close enough to the race in terms of time or are enough of them to build up sufficient acclimation to make a large amount of heat difference. The science advises you should be exposed for about an hour, two or three times a week to build up the best changes in your body. These changes fade with every week that passes without you using them in the heat.

It is worth noting there is great benefit to be exercising in the time you are being heat exposed. Heat chamber sessions do this nicely. My sitting in the sauna in my gym, less so. There is probably a lot to be gained from wearing everything you own, putting a pack on and then trying to run a half marathon. Or more. That should make you plenty hot enough.

I tried very unsuccessfully to make my own heat chamber. I borrowed an exercise bike, I bought a powerful fan heater and set it all up in my study. I bought a desk thermometer and blocked the gaps under the door with a towel. I managed to get the temperature up to about 34 degrees (93F) but no higher as the safety thermostat stopped the heater from working. I managed to sweat a bit on the bike but achieved very little. I gave up after only a few sessions as I didn't believe it was being at all useful.

Commercially available heaters don't go above body temperature. I couldn't find any which would give me a fifty degree (122F) heat to exercise in. The only things which might have worked would have been the butane gas space heaters. The problem I foresaw with that, was apart from the cost, I was concerned about the levels of carbon monoxide they might produce in a closed space. Carbon monoxide is a colorless, odorless gas and can be fatal. It produces unconsciousness as a relatively early symptom and is a silent killer.

* * *

You can of course do no heat training and simply turn up. You arrive a day or two before the race and spend a day out in the desert before the race starts. Unless you are after a top fifty finish, this may well be perfectly adequate and the complex measures tried by other people are probably not all that much help anyway.

Fluid management

Something as simple as drinking water has been made to seem frightfully complex in the last few decades. We used to drink when we were thirsty. Now we are are often told to drink a certain amount and to drink special liquids and that being dehydrated is terribly dangerous and bad for our performance.

Drink when you are thirsty.

The sports drinks industry has had a vested interest in presenting skewed, biased data to support the notion that we should all be buying expensive sports drinks. They have very big budgets and pay for very expensive adverts to convince the public, us. One of the **myths** is in the glucose content of drinks. Water, it turns out is just fine. Another **myth** is that you must drink before you are thirsty. Answer - wait until you are thirsty, then drink. If you are still thirsty, drink. When you are not thirsty, don't drink. It really is that simple.

There is a similar debate over electrolyte replacement. The main electrolyte to replace is sodium. There is no compelling evidence I have read for using any others. Your food will provide all the rest you need. There are a lot of expensive brands trying to make money from supplements. It is probably worth treating adverts and packaging claims with a pinch of salt.

When we sweat we lose salt. When we are heat adapted we lose less salt. Everyone's sweat rate will vary. The highest sweat rate I was able measure on myself was one and a half liters per hour.

Our diets contain a vast amount of salt in the region of ten grams a day. The amount of salt that you will lose in your sweat is probably in the region of about six. It is possible the salt capsules handed out on the MdS have no benefit. There is a paucity of robust supporting science. The organizers recommend we take a lot of salt capsules. While this may be helpful I feel they are too generous.

Nearly every race day I simply threw my salt tablets away. I didn't believe they were needed and felt them to be unnecessary weight. I took six salt capsules on the long day on finishing and was given two electrolyte tablets. I was feeling unwell and wanted to try anything. I'm not convinced it was an electrolyte balance I was suffering from but I ate what I was given. My tent mates were caringly feeding me and giving me lots of fluid, undressing me and positioning me for rapid recovery. They did sterling work and I am very grateful.

Some runners think cramp is is due to an imbalance in electrolytes. The science doesn't support this. Taking salt tablets upon getting some cramp is not going to be effective within seconds as is frequently claimed. We don't fully understand cramp yet, but there is spasm of slightly damaged muscles as part of a protective reflex. Using the limb differently so the other muscles groups or bundles can take over can be helpful. Stretching of the affected muscle is helpful too.

I thought that I knew better than the very experienced and

kind organizers about my water requirement. I didn't believe that being dehydrated affected performance within a few per cent points. The common citing is that if you lose 2% of your body weight though dehydration, this translates into 20% loss of performance. This has been refuted and was based on a poorly written study paid for by a sports drink manufacturer. There is some evidence that elite athletes win races when fairly dehydrated and clearly this didn't affect their performances. This was great in theory though the reading I had done was based on studies of elite athletes. I am not elite, not by a long chalk.

Having read about water ingestion and hydration, I wondered if I could run well, drinking less than others. This I reasoned could give me a competitive advantage. I would carry less water and thus less weight. I wouldn't be completely hydrated and thus would weigh less. If I could achieve this and maintain my best running then I would have a better power to weight ratio and would hopefully perform better in the final rankings. A cunning plan, but did it work? Not really.

I tried during my training to see how dehydration affected my performance in terms of minutes per mile and perceived exertion rates. I weighed myself before and after training runs. I calculated my water loss and thus sweat rate for various different running conditions. I found my sweat rate (through sweat and breathing) varied from three quarters to one and a half liters an hour depending how fast I was running and the ambient temperature.

My water loss rate also varied with how much I weight I was carrying. At 7% dehydration (over four liters loss) I started to get a significant loss of speed and it felt really unpleasant. At this level I was also more sensitive to lower sugar levels. This makes sense to me and could be easily counterbalanced by drinking to thirst and having a steady level of sugary foods during the race. It is of course a subjective study of one. Which is pretty bad science whichever way you look at it.

In the MdS, I set off with less water in my bottles than many others. I tipped water away and deliberately ran at about what I estimated to be two to four per cent under bodyweight. The advantage I hoped to gain here was weight. If I wasn't carrying so much in the bottles, then I should be able to move faster. If I was two to three kilos lighter due to dehydration and was able to perform similarly, then this would give me a better power to weight ratio. I couldn't improve my performance strength at that late stage (all that was set months previously by the training I'd done, or hadn't done). But I could change the amount of weight I had to haul up and down the hills and dunes.

In retrospect I sailed a bit close to the wind on occasions and was over optimistic on my race pace. I thus spent longer in the sun than I had planned because of my slow speed. This meant I used more water by simply being out longer. I probably sweated more than I thought as the loss rate was harder to estimate as your front in the sun was always dry. I often ran out of water before the checkpoints and did slow down on occasions because of this. My choice to always take one bottle when offered two is something I would change next time. I would also not tip water away next time. I would still choose not to carry unnecessary water, but would pour it over me. This would provide cooling which can provide a tangible benefit in terms of performance.

Among my many errors were I underestimated how much heavier my race pack was than my training pack had been at the time I did all my measuring. I underestimated how much fat I had put on during my taper. I also underestimated the water loss through sweat in the desert when the wind was blowing. The race was a lot windier than I had anticipated.

Most days on the race I was fine and performed reasonably

well. I wonder if I would go faster next time if I drank more. The day that the wheels fell off was the long day. This is the day I was looking forward to most as I thought I had got a decent race strategy. I had a great race plan.

But while *planning is indispensable, on the battlefield; plans are useless* - as Dwight Eisenhower said (Supreme Commander of the Allied Forces in WWII). I hadn't figured on the vomiting and nausea I experienced. I got my drinking very wrong and simply didn't do enough. Having a few hundred milers under my belt now, gives me the perspective that I didn't eat enough or early enough. This took me from a position aiming for 100 (or better, I am of course naturally a ridiculous optimist even in the face of lots of contrary evidence) to about 350 that day. This spoiled my plans immensely. No damage was done and my tent mates did a sterling job of patching me up afterwards and making me better. But I did feel like a bit of an idiot. Not to mention the difficulty of trying to run the last twenty miles when a slow shuffle was all I could manage. All I felt for those long long hours was the perpetual ghastly feeling that I was constantly about to be sick but could not manage to actually vomit.

nine

Back at the bivouacs

Each races differs with its version of luxury desert accommodation. In the MdS we were put up in black open sided tents called bivouacs. These are traditional Berber style tents. Each morning you are awakened by the Berbers throwing the roof off your tent. You are left blinking in the early morning sunshine. On a typical morning the air is coolish and you may want your long sleeved top on. Morning tasks include packing up your gear, having breakfast, performing toilet functions, your sunscreen and getting into your race outfit. You need to ensure your number is prominently and correctly displayed and the electronic transponder / GPS tracker is strapped securely. Then collect the day's water rations and make your way to the start line.

The queue for water is easier if two people from your tent take everyone's water card (they are stamped each time you collect) and carry the bottles back nestled in their arms. I chose to get my food in to my digestive tract as early as possible in order to get my toilet trip done before the queues mounted. I prepared my breakfast (skimmed milk powder, porridge oats and water) the night before in a water bottle. All I needed to do when I rolled out of my sleeping bag was cut the bottle down to size, voila: instant porridge in a bowl. Just like magic. Cold porridge. Which looked and tasted a little like a cold and rather oaty slurry. Yummy yummy.

Ear plugs for night time come highly recommended. I had six out of seven of my companions snore. None were overweight, so I regard myself as really unlucky. Tubby individuals are disproportionately more likely to snore, though many do not. The plugs helped a little. I took the expanding foam ones as they are lightest. Blue tack is cheap and works well, simple wax ones are good too. The best place I found to buy mine was my local village pharmacist. The major supermarkets typically had only one type to choose from. I experimented with and tried about four different types before I went. I do know this level of obsession marks me out as being a little weird, but my oddness may save you some time and effort and I'm happy to be of service. At least I have a little insight. Well I do now. And the medications seem to be mostly working.

Camel Spiders

I'm not a fan of creepy crawlies. They make my skin prickle and I'm not very brave. Luckily there aren't many creepy crawlies in the desert because there isn't much of anything living. There are a lot of flies although there was one photo by a tent mate of a scorpion. This he took on a rock face I had already scrambled up earlier that day. So presumably I had simply passed it by without noticing. I can't say that helped my uncomfortable night's sleeping.

There are also camel spiders in the desert. I've seen photos of these large spiders from other years but didn't spot any myself. I am glad as I'm not really an arachnophile. I'm told they have four lips each giving local anesthetic as the spider grazes - My room mate told me how during a military operation, one of his buddies was attacked and lost a significant percentage of his face during the night. Camel spiders are apparently not nice creatures. He recommends a routine check of your shoes each morning and inspecting the tent flaps at night. I'm not sure if this is real or camp-fire scaremongering …I'm just saying.

Emails out

On the MdS at 15h00 each day the email tent opens for business. A short while before there is a steady stream of runners hobbling toward the tent to form a relatively orderly queue. Some of the British competitors join the queue just for the love of queuing, to conform to international stereotype. This queue slowly roasts its victims in plain sight in the heat of the day. Though the end result of the queue is a lot less painful than the queue for Doc Trotters which starts to form about the same time.

Here, the sick and the lame of the desert gather to have the flesh flayed from their feet, to be anointed with iodine and have the holy zinc oxide tape applied to their war wounds.

The email tent has about fifteen or so terminals and comfy chairs where each competitor can send a single short email to one person of their choice. A bit like your one permitted phone call after being arrested.

Upon entering the sublime shady coolness of the tent you should select your terminal carefully as many seem only to have part of their setup functioning. I think it's amazing there can be any of them functioning in such an inhospitable environment.

You face a rubber keyboard a bit like on the old *Zx-spectrum*, there are a few f-key functions to press and *voila*, electronic mail. Some organized people type a day report and get the recipient to post this to their blog. This way their race sponsors can be availed of their progress. Rather unimaginatively I mainly used mine to whinge to my wife about how much my legs hurt and how it was hot and sunny again.

Checkpoints & cams

At the MdS there is a strong media presence and multiple monitoring of your progress for the outside world. 2015 saw the first use of the GPS transponder.

The finish line webcam isn't the only method your friends, family, stalkers and work colleagues can keep tabs on you and follow your progress. Once the race is underway there are a series of updates. As you pass each checkpoint your ankle transponder records your crossing of that particular waypoint. This information is fed via satellite uplink and updated on the website with a time and race position for each checkpoint that you pass. This happens in near real time. There seems to be a twenty minute delay. I think the delay is because the information is collated and bundle transmitted about every twenty minutes. Or so I was told. Maybe that was the emails.

Your progress will be shown by race number and is available on the official MdS website. This is available in both English and French. If you happen to find it in the wrong language you can click on the flag symbol and it will display in your chosen tongue. And there is now a pretty map of a lot of sand and your colored blob making its way along the course.

* * *

Apparently monitoring of the progress, checkpoint times and watching the finish line webcam becomes quite an obsession with those back at home.

Emails in

On the MdS every day there are deliveries of the day's emails. These are printed off and cut into short pieces of paper bearing the missive. These are brought around to each tent by the national representative. A bit like a Miss World in khaki shorts. Only different.

This visitation is evening's highlight and an occasion for much jollity, frivolity and banter. This is where your extended fan base from around the world send you messages. The messages arrive about a day after they are sent and typically congratulate the competitor on how they've done some 24h previously, so can seem a little disjointed.

Anyone can send one. Simply log onto the race website and click on the 'write to a competitor' link. All you need to know is the race number or name.

These were more welcome than I would have thought before the race. It is important not to be the only one in your tent not to get a message. That is a sad thing. So, before you leave on the plane, you must give your Mum clear instructions to write frequently. And possibly how to access the internet.

* * *

It is worth noting that many of these messages are read out loud, sometimes to the amusement of all. Accordingly, please include lots of embarrassing pet names along with honorable mentions for the other tent mates, this will probably go down very well.

Tent flags and mascots

Two of my tent mates were brothers and as British as they come. One was a futures trader and the other a marine. They not only brought their own body weight in terms of food and packs (which were progressively jettisoned as the days passed) but they brought along a Union Flag. This was raised at the end of each day when the last competitor from our tent arrived home.

In the afternoon when we had finished the race for the day, there was time to relax, eat some food and put the world to rights. One of my tent mates, being a professional tennis coach had some great stretching tips. He had brought a couple of taped together tennis balls for the occasion. These served as a do-it-yourself massage roller for the ileo-tibial band. They also served for a communal game of catch. Unfortunately this was sometimes a game of occasionally drop. The impacts of the drops proved too much and the tape ball was sadly no more.

During a chat about the weather with a work colleague recently, I am after all very English, it transpired he also had completed the MdS a few years before. His group of friends between them carried an entire cricket set; *stumps, bails and all.* I'm very impressed. It must have been splendid to watch a game of cricket played in the desert to the backdrop of dunes and the Saharan sunset. I only hope one of them had remembered to take along the Pimm's.

The good housekeeping guide

Upon returning to your tent after each day's race you should perform your daily housekeeping duties. This means doing what it takes to look after yourself and get your things in order, ready for the next day. This includes rehydration, stretching, nutrition and foot care.

Inspect your black toes carefully and establish if they might have liquid blood underneath. A subugual haematoma. This solidifies after about four to eight hours. If there is liquid present under pressure, this may be eased but the making of a small hole.

A needle is slowly rotated and the nail drilled to make an exit hole for this blood. Alternatively it can be heated in a flame until the tip glows red hot. Poke this through. This is quite safe - though may smart a little if you press a bit hard and puncture the underlying nail bed. This is all splendid fun and provides minutes of tense sweating for the squeamish while being a fascinating spectator sport for you, your tent mates and any curious passers by. A wimpy alternative is to go along to Doc Trotters (the race medics) and ask them to sort it out for you.

Another part of tent maintenance is to keep on top of your

trash and not let it blow around in the ever present winds. A bin liner is proved to collect all the debris and these are collected and whisked away each morning. This is possibly the only campsite in the world where there is a daily refuse collection. Having attended to general tidiness and your toes, your next task is to try to keep the sand out of your supper, your bed, your pack and your undies. After a while you may start to accept a layer of sand in everything and just yield to the slightly crunchy nature which enhances most of what you eat.

The more organized tenties will lift their mat on arriving back to groom the underlying desert floor. Sweeping for stones can seem a bit dull, but at three in the morning it can seem worth the effort. An effective way to do this is to use a long stick. Handily, the tent is held in place by just such sticks and they can be put to active service on this task.

Large stones should be retrieved from the adjacent desert and used to hold down the edges of the tent to help stop the wind and sand from doing its worst. At night, they keep the breeze out and the heat in. It is worth noting that the heat being kept in comes with a price-tag. Eight sweaty people who haven't washed or changed their clothes are sleeping in the space of a super-king sized bed.

This air can seem quite fragrant, aromatic even. Hanging like moist Jurassic mist and laden with a leaden heady aroma. Maybe the word should be *feety*. It should be added that many will be passing wind in the time honored fashion men adopt when in a confined space. It may be necessary to maintain some ventilation, purely for safety purposes. If you have an all-female tent, I'm sure this won't carry the same explosion hazard.

Aware of the risk of understatement, the smell of competitor's feet can be a bit unpleasant. Like a cesspit pongs and niffs a little in the heat of the summer. However it is surprising what you get used to. I was astounded at how eyewateringly unpleasant the stench was during the coach ride for the journey back to civilization. I struggled to breathe properly. I'd not really noticed the olfactory insult for a whole week before that point. The smelly assault on the nostrils is pungent but somehow strangely sugary and sickly at the same time. Like the Devil's sweet n' sour. A little bit like a warm fetid steaming compost heap. I suppose a manure heap is constructed in very much the same manner as the conditions we were brewing in our shoes. Debris, dead tissue, damp sweat and lots of heat. Nice.

Not everyone was as dirty as each other. In our tent, we had one chap who insisted on a clean shave every morning. He said it made him feel more human and carrying the weight of the razor was worth it. One of my tent mates carried a small flannel in a plastic *ziplock* bag. He used this for his daily ablutions. We had plenty of water and he was able to get quite an effective bird-bath each day.

Doc trotters

Unique to the MdS, Doc trotters is the name of the group of doctors and nurses who think it is fun to give up a week of their cherished annual leave to come and tend to your smelly feet. Other races have their own version, I imagine the themes are similar.

They are saintly for their patience and are welcome for their expertise. Your blisters will be popped and summarily sterilized with an iodine solution that **doesn't hurt at all**, no not really, no that's not tears of pain running down my face, they are tears of joy at what a neat job you've done for me doc. White tape is then applied to the offending area and does a remarkably good job of staying in place. All of my tent mates seemed to enjoy this process so very much that they dutifully joined the doctor queue at the end of each day's racing. Hoping, I suspect, to get one of the pretty ones.

In addition to blisters, the doctors deal with the various injuries and illnesses that elite athletes sustain at a race in the desert. Also the injuries that a thousand or so complete amateurs can come up with. Being mainly French-speaking it is sometimes not really clear what they say. I advise that if you are in doubt, simply lie down, take your medicine and say *'merci'* once they shoo you away.

In conversations with the medics it seems they are a diverse bunch, with many coming from emergency departments all around France. I was pleased to chat to a charming (meaning he spoke excellent English) cardio-thoracic surgeon. I'm even more pleased in turn that he didn't get to use his highly specialized skills on me.

Mad dogs & Englishmen

Mad dogs and Englishmen famously queue up in the midday sun.

Beware of the hot queue. You may be in one for up to an hour. Queuing in the UK is easy, you aren't usually in extreme physical pain and the temperature is not likely to be well above forty degrees. As recorded in the shade.

However, this queue is in the sun and you aren't moving fast to generate your own cooling breeze by your impressive turn of speed. You have a good statistical chance of feeling ill in the queue for emails or the doctor, as many do actually faint and collapse. I was never quite sure if this counts as queue jumping though.

The thorns of the bastard bush

This colorful nature-naming apparently originates from the British army and their encounters during peacekeeping duties with indigenous flora and fauna in exotic locations around the world.

There are in the desert many thistles and thorns, the camp is sited in this very same desert. Therefore in the camp perimeter there are likely to be many thistles and thorns. And indeed there are. You will also see lots of happy campers wearing hotel slippers as they are nice and light to carry. A downside of this footwear choice is that some of the larger thorns go right through these. Unless you have excellent eyesight and enjoy a state of constant vigilance you may come to regret this choice.

I elected to use my running shoes to wear around camp each evening. I modified them a little, so wore them without socks or insoles to make it shade more roomy. It is of course possible to pack light shoes such as the popular brand *Crocs*. I was on quite a mission to minimise weight, so took nothing extra. This was mainly so I could take a lighter pack. I sacrificed a degree of comfort and would make this abstemious choice on the next go around.

* * *

Towards the end of the week as I became more lazy and more accepting of the state of sandy grime in which we lived, I left the insoles in. This was because I was too tired to be bothered to take them out and simply loosed off the laces and crushed the heel the way my Mother used to tell me off for.

This choice of evening wear worked very well for me and I had no thorn concerns. I even kicked a few small rocks without incident. I would definitely do this again (not the kicking of the rock, that wasn't deliberate. I miss them a little now and will aim to miss all of them next time). The *x-talon*'s heel sprang and returned to its original running position each morning without incident. Having something safe from the thorns and pointy rocks to easily slip onto my feet was important to me in the middle of the night, as I typically needed to sally forth for a comfort break. These would be taken at about four o'clock each morning as my kidneys and bladder liked to show off by demonstrating how well they could perform even under extreme conditions. The double act of the kidneys and the smooth muscle of the bladder together conspired to get me up under the starlight each night to show me how well hydrated I was. Lucky me.

Constant winds

I wondered on the way round if the constant winds you find in the desert are similar to the Antarctic katabatic winds. These winds blow permanently, flowing away from the pole, often at over a hundred miles an hour. It seemed to me that we had something similar, presumably blown from the nearby Atlas Mountains. I now suspect they are simply a grumpy runner's perception of there being a perpetual headwind, when actually the wind comes and goes, much as it does nearly everywhere else on the planet.

For whatever arcane reason, it seems there is nearly always wind. On one hand, this is good because lots of stuff you need drying will dry. It is bizarrely nearly always in your face while you are running. It may be worth considering that you can run more efficiently if you learn drafting techniques like the cyclists do on the *Tour de France*, where they tuck in behind someone in front and let them do all the hard work against the wind resistance. Or take along your own *domestique*.

The winds affect not only your running but also life in camp back at the tent. Sand is blasted at you as if by a hairdryer with the setting stuck on hot. Swirling eddies carry golden grains into every, nook, cranny, crevice and crack along with each and every bodily orifice for good measure. Despite the heat of the day, the wind can become quite cold at night and when you are tired it can feel a lot cooler still. It is worth taking care not to actually become cold, applying layers is the best way to keep warm.

Having the tent arranged well is crucial for comfort. The sides and the flaps can be adjusted by rearranging the sticks used to keep it in place, sometimes quite dramatically so the shape is better suited to the prevailing wind and to how much you want to keep heat in or out. Often the sticks of neighboring bivouacs seem to be better than yours. Jealousy ensues.

At the camps on the MdS there are helpful men in blue caretaker overalls (Berbers) who are on hand to help, though you may have to wander around to find them. They are really good at pegging down and arranging the canvas on at least one side to protect you and your gear from the wind and the sand. In addition to Berber, they speak Arabic but understand French well too. They conversed with the Brits with the universal strategy of speaking your own language and waving your arms a lot.

I strongly recommend working closely with your tent mates to lift the carpet at each new site and systematically sweep the hard rocks from underneath where you will be lying. We didn't do this as much as we should have and I will be more proactive another time. It's not at all difficult, and with two or three of you, a great job could be done in about fifteen minutes. You do actually have fifteen or so hours in which you have nothing to do but rest so there are few excuses not to get on with it. Having a minimalist sleeping mat I stood to gain the most here, but you may be able to use the argument that tent life will be better for everyone if none are you are sleep deprived. Failing that, bribery with snacks or menial favors may be needed.

* * *

Trying to keep the perpetually blowing sandy wind out of the tent seemed at times to be an impossible task. We found it useful to hold the coarse black material onto the floor with locally sourced ballast. Small rocks abound in the desert, I know this to be true - I kicked nearly all of them.

Finding some medium sized rocks to place on the remaining flapping edges is best done early in the afternoon. Within walking distance there are only going to be a certain number of rocks. There are well over one hundred tents. Every afternoon there are men wandering about in flip-flops and *budgie-smugglers*, picking up and gathering stones in the sunshine.

It will serve you well to ensure your tent is as well held down as it can be, as you are going to be the one with decent and comfortable rest. I'm pleased to say that rock-envy didn't get the better of many competitors and there wasn't too much migration of rocks from yours to neighboring tents.

Luxury item and arachnophobia

Given my lack of love for spiders and other crawling beasties, I decided my **luxury item** was to be a bin-liner. This fifty gram black plastic refuse sack was to carefully place my shoes in each night. With the aim of inserting my feet each morning in the safe knowledge there would be no scorpions or spidery surprises awaiting me. Feeling suitably smug I proudly announced my plan to my new tent mates. An error of judgment.

My tent mates in turn duly promised to place any eight legged visitors they encountered into the above mentioned bin-liner. This news did nothing to allay my arachnophobia.

I heard no suspicious rustlings during that first nervous night. After the second night I discovered a large split in the liner and soon forgot about my worries as I then had no choice.

I'm told the only spiders locally are camel spiders and despite them growing up to 10cm diameter (body, not including the legs) they aren't apparently dangerous and would only give you a nip. I didn't get the horror story about the half-a-face thing until we were on the way home.

* * *

The only information on scorpions I could find before I went, told me that in all environmental niches on the earth there are scorpions but only seventeen of the species are poisonous to humans. I didn't find this very reassuring as you only need *the one that bit you* to be poisonous for it to be an issue and nowhere seemed to be able to tell me if South-Eastern Morocco held anything nasty. The only other help seemed to be cinematic research from watching films like '*The Mummy*' and I think that was set further East in Egypt. It was also not real. Probably.

ten

It is a race

Things which will get you round faster:
- how fast you can run
- how long you can keep that up for

Things which will hamper you:
- weight carried (you, your kit, water, nutrition)
- illness
- becoming grumpy
- pain and injury

Optimizing this is all part of the fun and the challenge over however many weeks and months you have left. If you only have days, you have my very best wishes - stop reading and go to a nice café with friends, there's probably nothing more you can do at this stage!

The elites - how they do it

The elite runners at the MdS have differening strategies. Many live and work in Morocco and the surrounding regions. For them, they have the advantage of being able to train in the heat, to practice on the terrain, to run on sand to recce some of the course and so on.

They are used to eating and drinking in the heat. They have the opportunity to try out the terrain and to see how their body reacts in training, and will have good prior knowledge as to what is needed in the conditions. Many of the elite runners have run the race before. This will also give you a pretty good idea of what to expect. So a top five finish for me next time … No excuses (*I'm kidding of course*).

Event specific training is much talked about in sport and in ultra-running in particular. If you want to emulate the elites, then take a month or two off from work and start practicing out in the desert. Or simply enter year after year and work on your performance and approach to the race.

The top runners can make serious mistakes with their race plans and things go wrong for them too:

2012 - *Favourite man* - serious muscle injury towards the end of the 80km leg, pulled out of the race.

2013 - *Favourite lady* - retired after leg 3.

The fastest British runner so far is Danny Kendall. Even faster than James Cracknell and he was pretty good. He has had to date, six goes at this and has now finished fifth, which is a fantastic achievement. It turns out, as should come as no surprise that his success probably isn't entirely down to luck.

Danny does have a few things on his side. He is in his mid-thirties. Meaning he is young and fit but with years of experience and the mental tenacity which comes with time (this is a great age for an ultra-runner). He too has an understanding wife. He has an understanding boss (who is often out of the country). He is a fantastic runner. His 5k, 10m and marathon times are enviable. He has the endurance of Sir Bradley Wiggins. He has the tenacity of a ship's terrier with a plump juicy rat. And he has a beard.

Actually, I'm not sure how the beard helps, but it is a feature. Mr Kendall works as an accountant, though seems to manage his time well enough to spend a lot of his day training. He tries to **train twice a day** for the preceding five to six months. Two out of three of; before work, lunchtime and after work. About an hour for each session. He does about one weights session a week and tries to do quite a lot of fast running.

He apparently doesn't do too much of his training with a heavy pack, and uses his exercise bike at home to do some cross training, which means he's able to spend this time close to his young family. His hill training is limited as he lives so close to London, though this doesn't seem to hold him back. In addition, he races. A lot. Nearly every weekend for months before the MdS. He also seems to win most of these.

* * *

Being adept at numbers, he is apparently fond of scrutinizing and studying his training and racing data in detailed spreadsheets. Attention to the intricacies really pay off for him. It may be the main benefit in paying attention to the small print is in maintaining the motivation needed day after day. Especially when the going gets tough. And it is going to.

There is good science which backs up the progress of the expert. This attention to fine detail to provide feedback about performance modification in light of adjustments seems crucial. This is from studies of outstanding international performers across a range of disciplines. One theory surrounding excellence is that you do need some talent, but an awful lot of hard work. Not just any hard work. But carefully focused hard work with constant feedback available at the time or soon after. It is this rapid feedback which allows the expert performer to adjust his or her technique to improve still further.

I guess if you really want to do well, you could just copy him. My easy guide tips are for the slightly less ambitious. And you don't need a beard.

Eating strategies

Choosing your eating strategy can be tricky. One reason for this is you may not have done anything like this before. Plus, everyone is quite different and what works for somebody else might not work for you.

The good news here is that as long as you get plenty of energy in, it doesn't really matter too much what you do or how you do it. The main thing which will help your chosen technique is mental. So if you believe that you'll be ok, then you probably will be.

There are some scientific studies about performance enhancing with sugar. These were done on professional cyclists and were done to find out the optimum amount of energy needed to power the cyclist. It was found that a solution of glucose water every fifteen minutes helped power the cyclists for longer. This was the basis of my choosing jelly babies and how often to take them. This is also the science behind why gel companies recommend their schedule of four per hour.

Most athletes feel that eating four gels each hour produces nausea as they are so sickly sweet. Interestingly, the glucose solution used in the studies didn't taste very sweet (pure glucose doesn't) and there was an additional finding that simply holding the solution in the mouth and then spitting it produced nearly the same energy boost as when it was swallowed. Spit or swallow, it all seemed to help performance.

The reason for this boost is thought to provide evidence for the central governor theory of sports physiology. This theory proposed by Dr Tim Noakes states that your body is capable of quite a lot, but your brain (the central governor) carefully and constantly down-regulates your performance so your body doesn't break. The brain is thought to hold you back. From an organism survival viewpoint having this safety feature is a good thing as this means that no matter how hard you try, you will almost certainly come to no serious harm. The harm will be prevented by your body becoming tired, painful or faint and giving you an powerful stop signal you will find it almost impossible to ignore.

The thing is, the safety margin on the factory setting is too safe. **You are capable of an awful lot more** than the default setting usually lets you have.

One of the results of training is it shows your body that you can push hard and you don't die, so the next time it lets you push a little harder.

When you exercise, the brain holds back something in reserve because it doesn't know how far you have to go. So giving a taste of glucose to the mouth receptors tricks the brain into letting you go faster, as it anticipates that the actual calories from the glucose will be absorbed in the stomach in the next few minutes.

Holding back resources and energy bursts because the brain doesn't know how far you have to go, is one of the reasons athletes can produce a final burst of speed at the end of the race. At the end, or when you know the end is coming up, your conscious brain is aware the goal is nearly reached. This in turn allows the unconscious brain to take the brakes off a bit as it then knows it has adequate reserves for the rest of the journey.

When you first start running, this distance might be the last few meters before your front door. When you train over bigger distances you can find a burst of energy to power you over the last five miles. When you run even longer distances, this distance goes up and up. This is fascinating stuff and is all in your head.

Approach to injuries

Working out what you will do with injuries in advance can save some stress and headaches during the race.

- Will you stop and attend to blisters?
- Will you take your gaiters, shoes and socks off so you can tape any developing hot-spots?
- Will you simply ignore the pain until you cross the finish line and power on through regardless?
- If you have muscle pains, what are you going to do about it?
- Have you a handy mantra you've practiced to distract you from pain?
- Will you take out a photo of your children and focus on how proud of you they are?
- Have you any painkillers to take if the need arises?
- Have you planned your actions if you are suddenly overtaken by diarrhoea?
- Have you thought about the etiquette of where you will go and vomit if required? *Just away from the path*

is acceptable. For poop emergencies, you need to dig quite a big hole, or use a poop bag - and then carry it.

- Are you going to have toilet tissue in an easy-to-reach location for emergency situations?

Racing strategy

Choices, choices. What will be your race strategy? Have you thought about it? Will you go steadily? Will you perhaps just enjoy the scenery or maybe just run to how you feel. Run when you can and walk when you can't. Are you going to set off like a tortoise and plod steadily round, or are you going to hare off and see just how long you can keep it up for before slowing down when you run out of gas, but with at least a few miles in the bank?

My strategy for the forty-six mile long leg was going to be to take it easy for the first forty-five, then give it all I had. That didn't quite work out but I think the reasoning was sound.

One by one and like a limping lurching set of zombies in fancy dress, the racers amble towards the start line. The French, of course being typically the last to turn up, usually arrive eating something appetizing. They are the smart ones. As the competitors are milling in the starting pen, the temperature begins to rise. There is music playing over the loud speaker. A general air of excited anticipation builds.

Typically there are a lot of people limping and hobbling around. Blisters and stiff legs are very much in evidence. When most of the people have assembled, Jack Bauer climbs up onto a Land-rover and starts to address everyone in French with a lot of arm waving and general enthusiasm (maybe he isn't called Jack. Patrick could be correct).

Listening through the translation provides a surreal delay. Each morning there are several birthdays and the crowd then dutifully sings happy birthday in their own language. For reasons which remain obscure, most of the crowd selects different keys and chooses to use variable timings too. This cheery list of congratulations, hurrahs and ensuing cacophony readies us for our journey.

All of this is made more tricky to hear and understand by the helicopters buzzing overhead to effectively drown out any useful communication. I reckon that you can't get too stressed by these things and that it's best simply just to relax and soak up the atmosphere. There are various orchestrated cheers for the different nationalities as he announces the top race positions. He always mentions the top US and the top UK entrant. Their supporters cheer the loudest and this seems to add to the slightly unhinged carnival atmosphere.

When all the preamble is done. It is time for the traditional count down. The loudspeakers start blaring AC-DC's 'Highway to Hell' and at some point there is a countdown commenced and thus the race starts. Everyone shuffles forward across the start line and in the dust and the mayhem tries not to run directly into any of the many camouflaged photographers who crouch, wearing buff colored gillets, low down in the dusty sand near the start line. I guess this press hack hurdling is a sort of traditional desert sport in Morocco.

Then nearly everyone manages to break out into a run for the only time of the day, holds that pace for a truly magnificent three hundred yards, and promptly lose all of their tent mates and friends in the frenzy of a thousand identically dressed runners in the desert *with the deafening low flying antics of the helicopter. Then nearly everyone starts to feel the pain of running on the sand and stops behind the nearest piece of knee high scrubby bush to have a wee. Then nearly everyone walks for a bit. The race is underway.*

If you pace yourself well, you can run at a steady rate throughout your race. This takes a bit of practice. Practice at races in the UK and you will discover that you can be passing other competitors for the second half of the race. This adds an important psychological boost if you manage it. This is because it can feel pretty good if you are even a tiny bit competitive. This is your reward for careful pacing and a whole bunch of training miles. This is the reward for getting your behind into gear and into the gear and heading out of your front door in the cold and the wind and the rain.

You can be magnanimous and pleasant to everyone you pass, they like this, sometimes makes them feel better and you get to feel smug too.

Pacing yourself carefully is a much more efficient way of running than starting fast, running out of energy resources and then having to haul yourself slowly over the remaining painful miles.

Running ultralong distances is about running against yourself more than running against those around you. People are generally supportive and the camaraderie of long-distance running is one of the things that makes it one of the fastest growing sports in the world today.

Running for charity

The MdS is a race and is billed as such. However, its ethos is about being somewhere very special and taking part in a magnificent event. It is this aspect of the race which draws many competitors to enter and compete to raise money for a good cause.

Many people choose to dedicate the race to someone they know, perhaps who has passed away or who is unwell. They collect sponsorship from people to give to a specific charity. In this way, thousands and thousands of pounds are raised each year for good causes. The event organizers themselves donate large sums of money to charitable causes and now there is a solidarity day after the race proper is finished which raises still more money.

Lots of runners will tell you their specific story if asked. They find it motivating when things seem tough, to know they are part of a bigger picture and they are better off and privileged to be able to be part of this amazing event. It is inspiring to hear their stories and truly heart-warming to hear what they and their loved ones are doing for each other.

Directions

The MdS road book is a beautiful small book which would have made a great memento but needed to be studied for each day's route, instructions and points of interest along the way. I didn't manage to get mine secured into my pack without it getting tatty and sweaty. Which is a shame because it would have made a splendid souvenir.

If you do have the misfortune to become lost despite the magnificent and frequent large direction arrows to follow. If you manage to somehow miss the two foot large high-visibility signs that mark the course day and night, there are compass bearings of where you should be headed written down in the book and these are easily followed.

There are two maps provided, a stylized line drawing with helpful landmarks and a more traditional map. You may be aware when you use a compass there is true North and magnetic North which varies with how far you have traveled South around the globe (magnetic drift). The organizers have already thought of that, so all you need to do is dial the appropriate number into your compass and run along with the needle in the red arrow. This is surprisingly easy - though I was more confident having already tried it out in the UK in dense woodland beforehand.

Do pay attention each morning to the approximate course details (by perusing the road-book or the translated instructions). Knowing the distances to checkpoints can prove a handy psychological boost, plus there was one instance of the road book written instructions having a different compass bearing to the diagram. A little thought soon made it obvious which one to follow should the need arise, but I'm glad I did this in the tent over a leisurely afternoon snack rather than in the heat of the desert while tired.

The signposting each day was fantastic and you really had to work at it to get lost. In most of the other long races I've attempted one can be running for hours at a time without seeing another living soul. I rarely managed ten minutes on the MdS out of sight of anyone. This was a really good thing as I would have worried I'd taken a wrong turn. This is an unfortunate tendency I have on races in the UK. There could have been more serious consequences in the Sahara, as the stakes were higher in terms of overall safety.

Other runners

The other runners you meet are an amazing bunch. Chatting on your way round is one of the highlights of the event for many runners.

People come from twenty or so different countries and speak many languages. On everybody's race number there is a country indicator (in French) and your first name. Given that your race number needs to be displayed prominently both fore and aft, it means you can greet other runners as you pass each other by name.

Some people seem more receptive to these greetings than others. It seems strange and can still be a surprise day in and day out to have someone greet you by name in the middle of the desert. This can give an amazing mental boost when you're working hard (as you may well be).

I tried to say a greeting in the correct language as people came past, or I went past. Otherwise a cheery wave is all that is required. Learning a few greetings like the French for 'not too far now', 'it's quite warm today' and 'well done, old fellow, keep up the good work' - amused me, even if not the many French runners I treated to a cheery salutation. My grasp of other languages is poor, at best. I suspect they hadn't a clue what I was trying to say.

There are many people I spoke to (or tried to) on the way round. You get to know the people who run about the same pace with you as you spend hours passing each other in a leap-frog manner. You can have some amazing conversations, discovering that some pretty special people make it to the desert and each with their story to tell.

Music or not

Opinions in runners are divided about using music. The debate is raged on the letters pages of magazines, on blogs, on the trails and in the bar. Some find it helpful and motivational. Some find it a useful distraction. Some runners feel it impairs your interaction with the world around you. This not only impedes safety but detracts from the zen-like experience of running and **experiencing the world with all your senses in overdrive**. Having awareness of where you are and nearby hazards is important when training near traffic. Not doing so can be thought of as irresponsible and risky behaviour. It may be dangerous and poor awareness can lead to serious or even fatal consequences.

In the desert, the debate perhaps shifts to one about interacting with your fellow competitors. Some feel that with music you won't be able to fully engage your senses in this amazing part of the world and experience the race to its full.

It is widely agreed that talking to people on the way round enhances most people's experience of the MdS. Thus, your music may lessen that opportunity. I run regularly with music in the UK, but usually race without it. Many races in the UK and nearly all those run entirely or partly on roads ban music devices. As I can get a massive boost from my music, I took my iPod shuffle with me as it isn't very heavy and is pretty robust.

I managed to get about one hour of use on day one when was struggling. This gave me so much of a mental pick me up, that six miles from the end, I was able to stop shuffling and managed to run the remainder miles, overtaking some twenty five competitors in the process. I was singing my favourite tunes out loud and it significantly helped me, despite the aural pollution to the poor souls whom I passed. The sound of my singing cannot have been at all pleasant for them.

Having had such a pleasing musical experience, I decided I would save the remaining battery power for use on the long day when I felt this would be of most benefit to me.

The error of that decision was in not understanding battery life. In the heat of the dessert the capacitor of the machine drains faster than back at home and I only managed to hear another three songs. I have since discovered that the battery loses about twenty percent of its capacity per year that you own it. If you use and recharge your battery frequently, it loses this capacity (strictly speaking, capacitance) more quickly still. In the heat, this remaining functional capacitance is greatly impaired.

A way around this battery issue is to take a solar charger with you and the various connectors required. Solar chargers can be quite expensive and have a definite weight. Practically, it will also need attaching daily to the rear of your pack in such a way that it doesn't fall off.

One of my tent mates fixed his to the tent exterior each day when he got in from the day's race stage. There are a dwindling number of daylight hours at that point and this device will need to be secured against the tugging, blowing and whipping of the wind (he used clothes pegs, which proved very effective). You will of course be carrying safety pins with you as part of your compulsory kit. You may think that safety pins would be suitable for attaching items to the outside of your tent. Indeed, this could seem like a smart idea. The downside of this apparently obvious choice is that most people's safety pins simply weren't man enough for the job. They were readily bent by the force of the wind. Rendering them somewhat less useful as items of emergency kit.

One particular challenge of attaching a solar charger to your pack is that it needs to cope with bounce and shake of many hours in harsh conditions. The fixing in place will need some careful thought and pre-planning. I may do this on my next MdS but will think very carefully about the precise weights, costs and practicalities involved. I will compare this with the perceived mental boost.

Finish line celebrations

When you cross the finish line there is a mat to register your time, some officials to record your number by hand and then a giant inflatable finish sign. There is also an enormous inflatable teapot, which despite its initial anachronistic appearance, after a few days seems to blend almost unnoticed into the normality of camp life.

Crossing the finish line and arriving back at base is immensely satisfying each day. Just after the line there is a webcam that you may approach. I was quite oblivious of this until long after the race. This broadcasts a live feed each day and my comedy Gangnam style celebration dance on my first day was spotted by my wife. She wasn't impressed. My Dad-dancing should be probably be left behind closed doors for the good of all concerned. The live feed can't be recorded so if your crossing is missed then that glorious opportunity and fifteen seconds of fame is lost forever.

If you have a better line crossing celebration than I, you might make the final video or if you have a handheld sign you can try showing this to the camera. I'm told that one chap proposed to his girlfriend on the webcam after one of the stages. I've no idea if this was a successful strategy.

There is no sound and the quality of the picture isn't quite up to lip reading. You should perhaps bear that in mind when communicating anything particularly complex to the waiting world.

Immediately after the camera the tea-tent is available. Sultan tea is a race sponsor and there is a nice man who hands you a **very hot small cup of sweet mint tea**. This is surprisingly nice and you will end up looking forward to this treat on your way round. Although perhaps a cold stone massage may have been more welcome. You will the have to precariously balance this scalding hot cup whilst you produce your water card for stamping, you are then given three litre and a half bottles of water to balance as you perform the tight-rope-slow walk to your tent. When I say walk, most competitors seem to limp and shuffle like zombie extras in a bad horror movie. This exquisite feat of balancing will be executed in the heat of the day, limping, covered in dust after one of the hardest races you've ever run.

Checkpoint Charlie

Going through the checkpoints has some scope for efficiency. These can give you easy minutes of advantage on those around you. If you've ever seen a pit stop on Formula One motor racing or the transitions at an international triathlon you may get a sense of what the MdS typically *isn't* like. The competitors alongside, who you transition the checkpoint with, are often those who you feel you are racing against. Seeing these same people on the course each day can provide a valuable mental spur in trying to better them.

I wasn't anywhere near the elite runners but I still got a real racing buzz out of trying to outrun my fellow runners I saw around me on the course. I'm a little childishly competitive, it is in my make up. The checkpoint was one of the places I was able to gain a few minutes of advantage. Water is useful but water is also heavy. In big bottles it can be cumbersome. Getting it into your drinking bottles can prove a bit awkward too.

Running up to the checkpoint, water bottles at the ready with the securing straps loosened, water-card out and ready for stamping. Asking for only one of the two bottles on offer. Taking the liter and a half (1.5 kg) bottle, drinking the first third (250ml) in three gulps,

259

putting 750ml in your bottle, pouring the rest over your head, discarding the empty and powering through the checkpoint. This was my technique which compares with taking on the full three liters on offer, stopping to readjust your pack, taking on snacks and having a five minute rest in the shade.

I entirely concede mine was significantly less luxurious - but I was there in the desert to push myself to my limits and to race the hardest race I could. Also, it felt fun to try and make it as fast as I could. I was alone in my little competitive world. No one else seemed to be doing this as I was a long way off the front runners.

Some competitors felt they gained a much needed mental boost from the rest. That approach may not have worked as well for me as I would worry the benefit may have been lost as I saw my hard earned places slipping away from me with every few seconds that passed. I left the checkpoints up to two kilos lighter than many others. It's probably because I'm a bit weedy, I found it difficult to run holding two 1.5l bottles of water - due to general laziness, wimpiness and poor upper body strength. I'm not saying I had the best strategy here, but thought you might like to consider logistics such as these and the impact individual decisions will have on your overall race performance. If you are taking the racing seriously then every minute counts and every gram makes a difference - they soon add up.

Etiquette on littering

This is a really simple rule. Don't litter. Really.

It is one of the race rules and makes perfect sense. You are encouraged not to litter your water bottles by the race officials writing your race number on the bottles so they can be readily identified. The discarding of a bottle that is subsequently found carries with it a time penalty and rightly so.

Beyond

When you finish, you will have traversed a lot of challenging terrain, you will have pushed yourself to and beyond many personal limits. You will have had a pretty amazing adventure.

Completing the MdS, you will have run a hundred and fifty miles across Saharan sands. You will have completed about five marathons in five days. You will have completed an ultramarathon of nearly fifty miles. You will have raced at night and will have come through a number of personal dark spots to emerge victorious.

You will have made new friends and have new tales to tell to your old ones. Then your plane lands, you go home and this thing you had been working towards for so long is gone. What now?

Some people are bitten by the bug and want to return year after year. Some people never want to run again. Some people can't run until they are off the crutches they now carry.

What will this new future hold for you? With the sand still dusting the clutter of clothes strewn across your living-room carpet, will you be plotting and planning your next adventure?

Your next foolhardy, epic challenge? Certainly it would seem a shame to lose this fitness you have worked on. That you have built up and now proven through magnificent use. Your persistence and stamina may well have reached new levels. Will you let them slide?

Many people come to realize they are capable of more than they ever thought possible. Much more. This is an amazingly liberating feeling. Lots of people go on to try other extreme events. There are super challenging ones emerging at an ever increasing rate as ultrarunning increases steadily in popularity. As the years pass, more and more people are drawn to ultra distance events for the different challenges they offer from the road marathon or the holiday hill hike.

Some go home to sit quietly and lick their wounds. Some people want to get home and connect with those closest to them. Many people who've completed the race have done so at a great personal cost to themselves financially and in terms of time away from loved ones and friends while training and on the race itself. For them it is time to rekindle those relationships. For nearly everyone it will leave a lasting impression and lifelong memories of an unforgettable experience.

eleven

My race

The journey I had, in case you were wondering:

Day one

Day one of the twenty eighth Marathon des Sables. My race started slowly as I drank in the atmosphere. I'm not sure I knew quite what to expect, but soon I was two thirds of the way down the pack and having a pee stop one quarter of a mile in certainly didn't help my positioning. I quite liked being buzzed by the helicopters though. It made me feel like a proper athlete. Unfortunately, this feeling didn't last very long.

I hadn't really given much thought to tactics or racing lines. I decided to have a go at working my way up the positioning. The desert pan we were crossing had a fine crust formed on the surface and was studded by scrubby spiky bushes. I believe some members of the British armed forces refer to them affectionately as '*bastard bushes*'.

These bushes looked like they would lacerate my gaiters and shred them with a poorly selected step. This kept me on my toes. Nearly literally. That fine crust looked a bit like the surface of a chocolate brownie. Choosing the firmer parts of the crust to run on gave slightly better purchase and allowed *slightly* better progress. With a bit of effort I started to overtake the occasional person. If you judged the crust wrongly, you fell through. The fall wasn't actually very far and was only about an inch, but this meant you had to lift your foot another inch higher. When you are weighed down by a pack and the sweat is starting to run over the eyebrows and into the eyes, I had a feeling that one hundred and fifty miles later, those inches would probably add up. Finding your step on the crust was all very well but with seven hundred runners in front of me, thundering off into the distance like angry rhinos in pursuit of water (or a good party with free beer), there was pretty much only soft brown dust to sink into.

It was like running along in a humungous bowl of soft brown sugar. This was unhelpful in terms of managing any semblance of speed and not at all like what I had anticipated. Choosing a path closer to the small bushes gave a bit better traction, but this involved running up and down many tiny hillocks in quick succession. Everyone else seemed to take a sheep like approach. The sheep approach was quite popular during the week. For nearly everything. It involved simply following blindly the person in front of you and whatever route they took, you did too.

For finding the route across the desert, there wasn't much need of a road-book. There were over a thousand people heading in the same direction. I was never at the front (who'd have thought it). There were also vehicle tracks heading in the appropriate direction. There were many sign posts en-route and the people who had erected these had used vehicles to get to them, with tracks therefore to guide us. The checkpoints had also been set up by people in large vehicles which had started the day at the camp, leaving yet more tracks which all headed in the same direction. These tracks were pretty good clues to the direction we needed to head. I must mention the photographers, they seemed to be everywhere. They too arrived in trucks which handily produced tracks that one could follow.

Today the start felt pretty hot but nothing I couldn't manage.

The heat took its toll by simply being out in it for hours. There was simply no shade to find. I really hadn't figured how slow I was going to run as the weather warmed up and I continued to shuffle along.

There was a long series of tiny rolling dunes (about head height) which had the effect of sapping almost all of my reserves of energy just beyond the mid-point today. They were very pretty but I was reduced to walking for a long stretch here. My spirits were boosted by sharing this stretch with George, one of my tent mates. He pretended to be surly and tired to make me feel better. Actually he was simply great company and really cheered up my day. This was walking I hadn't wanted to do. It felt like I wasn't trying. But I was. I really was.

When I figured I had about four miles to go, I put my music on and gulped down a rather warm and sticky caffeine gel. This had the desired effect. I then ran along singing (I truly have no shame). In this section there were loads of chunky medium-sized rocks everywhere for me to jump over with my newfound energy. I bounced and bounded like an excited puppy. I even managed to largely disregard the headwind funneling down the valley between the two promontories in the distance. Passing between these, gradually overtaking people, I rounded a corner and saw a mile long straight section to the finish line. After a few more undulating small dunes the sandy earth underfoot became reasonably hard packed. I accelerated (a bit). I celebrated the line crossing with a silly dance and collected my first celebration hot tea of the week. Stuart was already home (another doctor, local to where I reside in the New Forest in the UK). The awesome fast running he managed today wasn't actually a fluke. He replicated this and achieved a top one hundred finish every day and eventually finished as the fiftieth chap. Good effort.

Day two

Day two felt much harder from the start. The birthday rituals of the starting pen were the same as the first. There was generally a more excited feel in the pen than on day one. Perhaps this is because on day one there were more nerves. I certainly enjoyed the morning ritual more. Knowing what to expect brings its own reassurance. Once we were off to the strains of AC/DC's *Highway to Hell* there was once more the shuffle and stampede with the familiar sand blowing around. Again there were randomly placed occasional photographers to hurdle. These photographers crouched close to the sand with *Nikons* clacking, clothed in their uniform of light camouflage khaki. Only their sunglasses enabled them to stand out visually from the desert floor. I wonder how many were crushed each day. I never thought to count.

As we flowed forward a new feature emerged. A significant number of us were suddenly lurching like zombies, as if from a desert *invasion of the body snatchers*. My legs, it turns out had pretty much ceased to function overnight and trying to coax more than an undignified shuffle out of them proved quite impossible. Amusingly, I as looked around, hundreds of other runners were similarly afflicted as we flailed our arms trying to propel us forward to cover the twenty of so miles until we saw camp again.

It was always a little bizarre to get up from your tent, run past an inflatable teapot, hobble through nearly a marathon of desert to encounter your tent again. Back home after passing the inflatable teapot and bouncy castle once more. There was your tent sitting there amidst the black circle, looking all smug. It had been whisked across the desert and rematerialized, as if by arcane powers. Replete with magic carpet. For me, this simply added to the slightly surreal atmosphere of the whole experience.

There were a lot of climbs today. I felt these were long and challenging, but I seemed to soak them up better than many others. I managed to shuffle past and overtake people for the entire day. Which was nice. With each climb comes a descent. I love descents. I can hop, skip and dance around other people on rocky descents and love to simply take the brakes off. Brakes off, brain off. I was taught this by another runner on a race in the UK (thank you Kris). He's much better than me now though and I see his heels vanish shortly after the start line when we race together. This flowing down the slope, working with gravity, works well not only on wet muddy winter trails but for the long sandy descents too. Plummeting down the big dunes of the race was quite the best fun I've had with my clothes on. Well worth the entrance fee alone (almost, anyway).

Stegosaurus ridge awaited us today. My name, I'm afraid. No one else will know what you are talking about if you mention it, though I suspect they may recognize the description. After a prolonged climb of soft sand and hopping stepping stones complete with multiple maddening false summits, we had a mile long ridge to navigate. To the left was a treacherous drop and a lot of fancy footwork was needed to navigate the thousands of rocks and boulders along this section. I was trying to keep my cadence up in the way I'd read was efficient and clearly I looked a bit of an idiot. An Australian voice behind me piped up as he had decided I was to be called *twinkle toes*. He proceeded to chat away in what I was to learn was the bombastic good natured humor which marked him out. We ran past each other many times over this and the next few days, with him cheerily calling out Twinkle toes each time he passed.

At the end of this rather technical section which had me swearing but that I rather enjoyed in hindsight, was our first major sandy descent. This was a fabulous one hundred foot drop with soft sand and no instructions. I arrived with no one else in sight. I felt like the route went down this vertical wall of sand. I realize it wasn't vertical, but it was very hot and my brain was starting to play tricks on me. I thought, in for a penny, in for a pound. I stepped off the edge and started to gather speed. Lots of big fast steps plunging up to my mid-thigh in warm soft sand as I hurtled downwards, protected by the same soft sand in which I was inducing mini-avalanches. It felt amazing.

Not soon after, we had a mile or two of heavy going (really soft sand) underfoot with a really awkward camber (left foot down), this was much harder than it looked and an alternating run-walk was very much the order of the day as I could manage nothing faster. I got chatting to a Geography teacher who was looking much stronger than I. He had a watch which apparently recorded the temperature at fifty degrees. Shade temperatures are misleading because you aren't in the shade. We had a three mile crossing of dried up lake to a checkpoint, where they announced the temperature to be a record for the MdS in the shade (I suspect they were trying to make us feel better). A lot of people were hanging about and trying to put off going up the wall of stone on the other side. This looked to be vertical from a distance, but as I approached it turned out to be a quite manageable bit of bouldering and clambering.

Not vertical then, it was just that the path ran up a reasonably steep section. It just happened to go up for half a mile. I was feeling good and decided to follow a couple of faster runners who seemed to be zipping past everyone else. So I overtook plenty and enjoyed this. It did get a bit narrow and I was held up by the general slow pace of those ahead. We had no choice here but to get our collective breaths back with a slow climb as we formed a queue snaking upwards. This section is where I later discovered the scorpion was sitting in quiet watchful anticipation.

There was a rope section at top. A piece of rope to grip onto and haul yourself up a steep sandy stretch right at the top, just before an apparent photo opportunity. A lot of these photo opportunities seemed to be at the top of a climb - where you tend to look sweaty and out of breath. Lots of photographers and helicopter action here. Apparently they go up this section every year. It's supposed to be tricky. I read later that Mohamad Ahansal had declared this year's stage two to be the hardest he's ever done. I'm not so sure.

For whatever reasons, I had a fabulous day. It was beautiful. I don't mind the hills and there were some awesome downhills to play on. I'm not very good at running fast so the downhill parts give me a chance to feel what it is like to be a fast runner. I think I'd enjoy being faster. It feels awesome to hurtle down a slope, at speed, just a little bit out of control.

After the photo opportunity at the top of the precarious rope section, there was a long technical bouldering descent. After a short rolling dune bit there was a mile long scrubby section and the finish line came into sight. Today I was first back in from our tent with a top 100 finish. The joy of this only lasted a few minutes and the only reason I'd arrived first was due to a torn gaiter issue necessitating running repairs for our resident fast runner. With the water bottles today I really struggled to balance my tea. Oh well. I was generally feeling fairly smug and pretty pleased with today's efforts.

Day three

Following our morning tent ritual of an octet of men farting and out-grossing each other, we donned our gear, gradually transforming ourselves into the ultra-athletes we tell our families about. The start pen was noticeably more jolly today as the pre-race nerves of previous days had faded. We had a job to do. We had to cross a lot of desert. But this was an achievable job. We had all done this before. We knew about running on sand. We knew about taking on water and salt. We all had day jobs back home but this was going to be a lot more fun. And you know what? It was forecast to be another sunny day. What splendid fortune indeed.

The helicopter dipped and swooped, the pilot seemed to be having as much fun as we were. The music blared, people jigged. Mr Bauer chattered away enthusiastically in French drowned out intermittently by the helicopter and plane. Comprehension was blunted as a result. A couple of race officials bustled around the competitors to ensure your race number was properly visible and not obscured by any straps. We ambled across the start line, the elites I presume ran, but I didn't see them. Mohamad Ahansal was shorter than me and I could barely see over anyone's shoulders. So I have to take it on someone else's authority that they ran majestically across the line, in sharp contrast to the more magisterial procession the rest of us were able to muster.

The limbs seemed to move a little better today and the lighter packs led to more enthusiasm as we collectively tried to kick or avoid French photographers in the dusty melee. The slightly lighter packs gave to more unpredictable movement as it seems that many of the others were oblivious to the idea of tightening down the straps each day. The challenge of jostling and jockeying for position in the early morning sun was compounded by the sport of *secret jousting*. Secret jousting is where a competitor with walking poles who clearly is going to spend the entire day walking, sprints away with the elites. Then they slow to a pedestrian walking pace once the dust clouds are in full force. The jousting and skewering commences as they start to randomly swing and jab their poles at anyone attempting to come past them. In their shiny sunglasses and staring fixedly ahead, they pretend not to notice when they skewer, kebab and joust those foolishly trying to overtake them. Such fun.

Today was a bit hot. The wind dropped and someone seemed to have the temperature dial turned up to full. All the way to eleven. The air conditioning didn't seem to be working today, maybe that was the problem. Today we met a couple of long picturesque stretches across some very smooth dry salt lake flats. These white salty miles were lovely to run on as you didn't seem to descend through the crust of sand we had become accustomed to. The ground seemed very flat and firm. The route was clear, there was no wind resistance. It was jolly warm though, so I still only was able to manage a sort of ambling shuffle. No land speed record attempt from me today.

Recalling Second World War action films I watched as a schoolboy, there were often dramatic desert scenes. Set in miles of beautiful rolling dunes and apparently mostly filmed where we were running. No wonder I had film set associations. There always seemed to be a scene involving a mirage of water that wasn't there. The heroes were hot, thirsty and had been driven half mad by exhaustion. In this sorry state, they hallucinated oases which weren't real, whole lakes of water that didn't exist. This never really resonated with me, I couldn't believe that someone would imagine such a thing, even when quite desperate. Well, maybe when death was almost there but even then most people maintained their sanity, didn't they?

Well, I was in for a shock today. About twenty miles in, we were crossing what seemed to be the hottest place on earth, a ten mile wide salt pan rimmed at the edge by distant mountains. The distance was quite hard to judge as it all seemed a little blurry. This blurring I reasoned was because of the air lifting as it was warmed by the sun reflecting off the baked white ground beneath. I vaguely wondered if my shoes would melt, though I'm pleased to report they did not. The ever present winds of previous days were absent. I was surprised and irritated to note that the perpetual blowing had been giving a significant cooling effect on previous days which I hadn't fully appreciated. This was highlighted presently because there was absolutely no breeze right then, nothing, zip, *nada*, not a puff and boy how I missed it.

Looking to my right I saw an absolutely huge beautiful blue lake. Shimmering gently with the sunlight reflecting off its invitingly cool surface. I was drinking in the view and admiring what a beautiful sight this was when a small quiet voice at the back of my head piped up to inform me that it wasn't actually a lake.

Not a lake? How ridiculous, of course it was a lake. I could see it.

'Nope, you are imagining it.'

* * *

Rubbish, it's so pretty and I'm not mad.

'Yup, it's an optical illusion.'

Caused in much the same way as a black-top Tarmac road can do this in the height of the Summer (something I'd noticed as a kid and enjoyed spotting from time to time since).

This was the same type of phenomenon.

For the next hour or so, this beautiful lake swam in and out of my visual focus as my brain continued to play mean tricks on me. I spoke to various other competitors about this, who agreed they saw the same thing.

I now wonder if they were humoring me and simple social awareness compelled them to take pity on this sweaty smelly Englishman who was babbling such nonsense as stuff about a mirage and a lake that wasn't there. Maybe I appeared rabid, was foaming at the mouth and was considered to be mildly dangerous. Like an unpredictable and slightly unhinged mangy terrier. I will never know.

There were some impressive climbs today and I again encountered a feature which you only really find on ultramarathons. When you get to the top of a long climb even during a hard fought race there are people standing around talking, eating some food and posing for photographs. Some are chatting away to their video diaries and it all has the air of a tourist spot on a nice Summer's day. But no ice cream.

The first five miles of the day had taken us through what passed for a busy city. Five or six low yellowing buildings without roofs. Rendered with smooth plaster which showed pockmarked crumble. The walls made dull by exposure to years of relentless wind and sand. The powerful wind was back and hairdryered into our faces during the whole of this stretch. I found three tall Norwegian chaps to follow here. They seemed to be running in convoy and running a little faster than I was managing, but I do love a challenge. The short train of three giant Norwegian locomotives had a short fat English bloke tag on top draft at the back. I ran close to the pack of a man whose name I couldn't pronounce and tucked my nose hard in behind. Matching their long loping strides, we danced in and out of the ruts and powered along into the wind. We hopped in and out of other competitors, leap frogging them (not literally, that would be silly) as we made steady progress into the powerful head wind.

The wind whistled past the small houses and seemed to have funneled from the very jaws of *Hades*. Hot, hard and filled with fine sand, it blasted at our faces. Eyes screwed up against the onslaught as we tried to find the best route to take. My routing choice generally consisted of picking my way up the long line of runners from one big bloke to the next. Tucking right in behind yet another tall runner with a big pack for me to use as a convenient mobile wind brake. Handily they all seemed to be going in the same direction. What luck!

There was a long valley which felt to be about ten miles long. This meandered and wound around like a huge fat snakeskin discarded and allowed to wither under the scorching sky. At one point I spied a few exhausted looking donkeys huddled around a couple of tiny trees in what passed for a modicum of shade. Their owner was apparently a lady clad in top-to-toe deep blue cloth. I couldn't be sure it was a woman. The general shape was fairly feminine, so I assumed. There was only a keen pair of eyes peering out. No response to my cheery greeting. I even tried some Arabic. No response.

* * *

Presumably she had taken some shelter on a long journey. A long fairly quiet journey I would imagine. And here she was, passed by one thousand curiously dressed noisy sweaty foreigners. I can only begin to imagine what she must have thought. No wonder she perhaps viewed us a little suspiciously. Perhaps she had whooped and applauded the first few hundred runners and by the time I passed, her hands had become tired and perhaps a little sore. Poor lady.

This long and winding river remnant was full of ridiculously soft sand. I tried and tried to find the best area of purchase. Repeatedly swapping sides and tracks in an endless attempt to try and find some more efficient places to put my feet as I could barely lever my pace above a walk.

To help pass the time there was an amusing game of invisible leap frog played by myself and some Spanish guy. We never spoke and he never acknowledged me. We were within eye and earshot for about two hours. No hint of my existence seemed forthcoming, so perhaps I imagined the whole thing. Nor did his TV crew acknowledge me. There was a presenter, a cameraman and a man with a fluffy furry microphone (which must have been fairly warm in that unseasonal attire). They ran alongside us, mainly him, for a hundred or so yards. Presumably trying to keep my handsome frame out of the camera shot for some unknown reason. We'd then jog on and they would leave us to find their vehicle I guessed. I never did see it. I'd forget about them and twenty minutes later, there they would be, jumping out from their hiding place behind a bush and the whole process repeated. It was really rather surreal. Though it was a nice distraction from my frustration at the deep sand. For a couple of hours there were just the five of us in sight under the azure blue skies and dazzling sunshine. Or maybe it was just me.

Day four (long day)

The infamous *Long day* awaited us today. For the front runners, this is where the race was won and lost. So they were given a three hour lie in and we got a head start. A bit like a prison break. The starting pen today was markedly subdued. By comparison with previous days, the atmosphere was one of apprehension and there were dark mutterings and quiet contemplation of the enormous task ahead. A full marathon. Then a half marathon. Then about another four or so miles to go. It didn't sounds so bad when you broke it into sections.

The camp looked slightly different today as the Berbers dismantled it around our ears. There were today a few tents left standing in proud splendid isolation. Here, the elite sat. The top fifty placed runners would today be attempting to catch up with the rest of us mortals. A massive game of tortoise and the hare. One thousand of us would be given a three hour head start and then the elite group would set off and try to overtake us.

It was supposed that this was for them a harder task as they would set off in the heat of the day. I'm not convinced. The rest of us would also be out in the midday sun, having run for three hours already and not having lounged around scoffing yummy snacks in the shade of a cool, naturally air-conditioned tent for an extra three hours of quiet rest, relaxation, recovery and generally kicking it back and enjoying the sunshine and the view. I'm sure you won't be too shocked to know that even with a three hour head start, we all were overtaken by the top fifty and soundly pipped to the post. They caught up and then overtook alarmingly quickly. They streaked past like we were walking. Err, lots of us were.

People weren't hobbling so much today. Fewer stiff limbs creaking. Maybe people had less DOMS. Perhaps it was just fear and being distracted by the prospect of a whopping ultramarathon. Who knows.

Today was my day for getting lost. I trundled along in my own sweet way. There I was merrily bimbling along. My few remaining functioning neurones concentrating fully on simply putting one foot in front of the other and generally trying to work out how I could go a bit faster to get me to the end, for my rewarding cup of tea and a sit down in the shade. Shade. I never realized how much shade isn't available when you could really do with it. The only way I could imagine to find some was for me to dig a hole in the sand and cover myself. I went on to reason that not only might this not be very cooling, but it most definitely wouldn't help me on my quest to move forward one step at a time towards the day's goal of finding base camp for a sit down and nice cup of tea. Did I mention tea?

And so it was with these thoughts swimming around my mind as the sweat swam in rivers down my back, that I looked up and realized I wasn't really on a trail and I couldn't see any footprints in the sand. Figuratively and literally. I had descended a gentle slope and arrived at a desolate looking dried up river bed running from right to left. On the other side there was a small bank and a rather dense area of head high gnarled dried husks of trees. My head is quite low, so the trees didn't need to be particularly lofty or impressive to achieve this. I couldn't see a way through. There seemed to be no path. The sand beneath me was all churned up and relatively soft and fluffy. No tracks could I make out. Bugger.

In case of times of panic such as these I had a pre-planned strategy. I implemented this like a well trained elite soldier. I stopped, I ate a couple of jelly babies, I drank some water and looked around. I then produced my compass and identified which direction was North and took my pack off to rummage around for the road book. I located the day's pages and although they were soggy with perspiration, falling to bits in my hands and difficult to interpret, I managed to deduce that I could be nearly anywhere from the start until the end. Oh dear. Everywhere does look a bit the same and all of the landmarks supposedly on the map had somehow escaped my attention on my way past. Fiddle sticks.

I did what any irrational chap would do in these circumstances. I drained my remaining water at an enthusiastic single gulp, clutched my compass, selected a heading and headed into the trees with an optimistic smile, hoping to meet someone. It wasn't, I admit, a great plan. But it was at least a plan, a strategy to follow. It was perhaps twenty minutes later that I heard voices. Feeling pleased my cunning plan was at last working, I made my way like an excited schoolboy to where I could hear the other competitors. When I emerged triumphant from twixt the gnarly trees, imagine my surprise as I was once more in the same dusty river bed. There was no mistaking it. Well done me. But now I got to share the experience with about eight fellow runners feverishly consulting maps and compasses.

Fortunately someone had been paying proper attention and was able to say where we were on a map. This then gave us a compass bearing to take and and a heading to head for. Off we set in convoy. This was on precisely the same heading I had recently chosen, so I should have stuck to my guns. Hey ho.

Having your name plaque emblazoned on your race outfit was, I think, so that when you are face down and generally incommunicado, that attending medical personnel can shout your name loudly during their attempts to revivify you. Your national country code and the name you are registered as, are printed in large friendly looking letters along with your race number. I was GBR 869 Phillip. This information was available both on the front and the back. This meant that this information was on everyone else's front and back too. A tremendous boon for people whose memory was as unsharp as mine. This sort of thing should be taken up by party hosts everywhere. I, for one, would be grateful. You can   pretend to recognize all sorts of people to whom you've only recently been introduced, but have no recollection or idea who they are.

On the MdS you are able to approach other competitors during the race, knowing both their first name and their nationality. You can choose if to greet and what preferred language to do it in. I had a lot of fun with this. Upon being overtaken, a quick glance over your shoulder enabled you to do the same. You can murmur words of suitable encouragement to anyone who passes, or who is collapsed by the side looking forlorn and thirsty.

Over the week, I got to say hello to the same MdS support team a lot. Didier and Francine often seemed to be stamping my card at the checkpoints and would enthusiastically greet me by name. Their exuberant greetings in heavily accented English would prompt me to shout back my race number in French at them. This was to facilitate their writing of the number on my water bottle. Then I would give them one of the few French salutations I know. I think they pitied the tired looking Englishman with the green stripe across his nose. But I had fun. They brightened my day and I looked forward to seeing which crew were at each of the checkpoints.

Water distribution was at the beginning of the day. You all queued with your water card. This was stamped and your bottles handed to you with your race number hastily scrawled on the top. At each check point, the same procedure was in place. Queue up, card stamp, number scrawled and bottle handed back with a grin a cheery Gallic good luck greeting.

As the heat of the day beat down I was gradually slowing up. Progressively I was becoming nauseated. I found it difficult to force myself to take sips of water and today's jelly babies didn't give me the sugar boost that I'd felt on other days. I had a small psychological boost when Salameh Al Aqra streaked past me and I cheered him on and tried to catch up with him for a while. This was rather optimistic of me and I nearly missed a whole load of ammonites and trilobites just lying around on the ground as I trundled across yet another dusty flat area covered in small rocks. It seem strange to think that only a few thousand years ago this region was covered in verdant swamps. With all the sand it was like the tide went out and had forgotten to come back.

The elite chaps trotted past in a line snaking off into the distance, taking what might charitably be called racing lines rather than corner cutting from the marked course. I was in no position to argue, watching their style was very impressive. My nausea escalated with the minute. Then the vomiting started. Legs apart, crouch down and try to stop my legs from cramping - which really didn't help the situation. An elite lady peeled off the track to come and offer me assistance; *are you ok?*. I wasn't looking at my best, so I waved her on (she had a race to win). I think it was Meghan Hicks, but I never did ask her. It was a really kind gesture as I think she was in the lead.

* * *

I didn't feel much better for emptying my guts and felt for the next five hours that I was about to vomit. It was a horrible horrible sensation. There was a pretty sunset which I remember vividly to this day. As the heat of the sun faded from furnace to simply very hot, the sky was full of pinks and reds and almost made me feel better. I was only able to manage a walk. Not even a fast one. I couldn't even jog for the nausea overcame me within seconds.

It was time for the glow sticks. I shuffled on into the next and last checkpoint. I'd decided that my race was over. I would let them ask me if I was ok, they'd call the medics and they'd take me away. I might get a drip and then I'd have given up on day four. That was ok, I'd tried.

Passing through the checkpoint. They asked if I was ok, I said no, they smiled and gave me my water and I walked past. There must be some mistake. They would have seen how ill I looked. I struggled to a rest bivouac. I managed a not very gentle face plant. I was hoping to be pulled off course. No one came. After forty minutes I sat up sheepishly and forced food and fluids down. I then shuffled off. Baby steps all the way in. I put on my tiny little head torch and realized quite how rubbish it was.

I was simply surviving. It sounds very much like a drama queen, but I could only concentrate on putting one foot in front of the other. My head was a giant bowl of gently whipped fish. My stomach churned and I teetered on the cusp of a puke for hours. I knew if I was on form that I could have run that last glorious flat section in about forty minutes. It took me I think about four hours.

Deep in my darkest hour, at the depths of my misery I heard a cheery 'Philip / Great Britain' as someone shouted out my race number details. I was being overtaken by the Mobbs brothers and the flag. They were looking strong. They passed me about three miles from home and beat me in by about two hours.

Limping for home, I'm not really sure why I was limping, that part is a little fuzzy now. What I do recall is that somehow I managed to be at the same pace as another poor soul who decided that I was ok to walk with. He did have a superior torch. I think I made a soft moaning noise with every step. For hours. I felt terrible. The lights of the finish were clear in the distance and didn't get any closer for a very very long time. Still we continued our slow shuffle in, our death march.

The famous laser seemed to be missing. It flashed on and off a couple of times, then nothing. That was a bit disappointing. I know that it wasn't deliberate but I had really been looking forward to closing in on camp brought ever closer by the glorious green tractor beam pointed towards the cosmos like something out of *Star Wars*. Never mind, I was too ill to really appreciate it. As I eventually crossed the line in arms raised celebration with that poor chap who I shared that journey with and who supported and encouraged my miserable ass all the way in. Thank you if you ever get to read this. I owe you some beers.

It was still jolly warm. Even in the night. Not quite sweaty warm, but then again I was being overtaken by snails. Even in my grouchy sphere of unwellness I was able to revel in the beautiful canopy of stars up above. No moon, but simply an amazing sky lit up with the full panoply of milky dots. I knew that I was properly privileged to be there. Still, I'd finished. Curiously I felt no sense of elation. Not even relief. Nothing. The nausea was still there, overwhelming everything. No tea for me today, I headed straight for the water and was spotted by my tent mates. They bustled around me. My pack was lifted from my shoulders. My water was fetched. They carried me and laid me down like a bloodied and bruised battle victim. My gaiters, shoes and socks were removed. I was fed wonderful drinks, snacks and nibbles and minute by minute I was revived. I slowly surfaced like a drowning man from the depths. I probably cried. I hope no one noticed. Two or three more arrived in what felt like the next few minutes and our tent was complete. We raised the flag in teary eyed ceremony. We'd done it. We'd all got through.

I was still feeling rough as a badger's arse as I went to sleep, but knew that it was all going to be ok, as this was a considerable improvement on my earlier state. More that that, I knew that the one remaining race day was doable. I was going to finish. We all were. I drifted off into a fabulous heavy velvety sleep. Sinking down in the comfort of my sleeping bag, no pain could I feel as I sank happily into the dark depths of slumber. Wow. What a day.

Day five (rest day)

Somewhat strangely I felt cured by the morning. The morning routine felt strange today. We had our breakfast as usual, but no Berbers bustled to remove the comfortable roof of our dwelling. There was no racing today.

We loafed and lounged around in relative comfort and ate each other's food in a giant game of swapsies. We tended to our feet, we mended our packs. We told terrible jokes. We watched the steady stream of runners still finishing. The day grew warmer and we enjoyed some sunshine without having to wear all of our gear. A bit of limping was seen. Quite a lot really.

Generally life was pretty chilled (in the hot sun). The day flew by for me. As is traditional, around the mid-afternoon mark, the last runner staggered in. The entire camp of over a thousand of us gathered to clap and cheer the tired but very relieved last quarter of a mile of this exhausted soul. I'd been sluggish but managed hours of rest and recuperation and a full night's sleep. There they were, still putting one foot in front of the other. A brave effort indeed.

Day six, race day five

Marathon day to finish. Just a quick 26.2 miles across the burning sands and scorching sky of the Sahara. What could be more fun? We had recovered and refueled all of yesterday and most of us were feeling pretty good. The task was achievable. We had survived a seventy kilometer race in similar conditions. We all knew we would finish, or so we thought.

All of this led to a pretty relaxed chilled start. The starting pen was filled with a real party atmosphere. It is one of the best race starts I've ever had. There was lots of joking and fun. Endless selfies and groupies. A few otheries (*like a selfie, but of anyone else*).

Setting off deliberately at the back of the pack, I decided to pace myself and try to reel everyone in during the second half. But it wasn't until the half mara point when I even started to overtake people. I later thought this pacing plan was a mistake. A mistake not to have wound up through the gears a little earlier. I was disappointed with my finish placing. Just from a competitive point of view mind you. The race itself was fabulous. I've never finished a marathon in such good spirits before. It felt awesome.

The day unsurprisingly was hot, it was very hot. There was a brisk headwind with soft going underfoot for the first ten or so miles, but I was trying hard and running with a steady effort. The problem for me and my silly competitiveness, was that nearly everyone else tried hard too. I had to put the power through my legs and crank the effort level up to eleven to actually start to make some headway. After an hour or so, the hard work paid off. As the sun climbed and the furnace heated up, I started to overtake a few people. The steady effort started to reel people in. Finishing in the top two hundred in about five and a half hours was my reward. I must have been a long way down the pack as I ran faster and faster towards the end. Actually I was feeling good for the last four or five miles.

The last couple of miles towards the magical inflatable teapot was a glorious steady downhill after passing through some ruins. The sandy deserted shanty town was like running through a film set. I imagined zombies appearing round every dusty corner. I suspect this was the heat. Perhaps after all the slow start was what I needed. I was even able to produce a sprint finish for nearly the whole of the last mile.

When I say sprint, I was probably doing ten minute miles rather than my usual twelvers. But I felt like a running god. At that point and with no basis in science I regretted not setting off faster. Never mind, the finish felt awesome (to me. In my head). Crossing that line is something else. Plus, I got a kiss from a jolly Frenchman. Monsieur Bauer, the race director and who's brainchild this ridiculous race is, with a beaming smile gave me a Gallic hug and kiss to welcome me home. No tongues, in case you're wondering. Mint tea next after forgetting to pose for all the photographers.

A pretty smug feeling. That was nice. Followed by a strange feeling which I hadn't anticipated. It was an empty awfulness of that finish line crossing being the end. The end. After years of anticipation, after months and months of obsession and training. After two hundred and fifty kilometers of Saharan sand in a silly hat. That was it. No more. I felt a bit hollow. I could have rather done with it being the same number of days again. Hmmm. Whatever could I do? Onto another challenge maybe? UTMB anyone?

Hobbling back to the now familiar tent with a big shiny piece of bling swinging from my neck and glinting in the sun under the glaring sky. I rested and ate. Stuart was already in. Obviously. Together we went to swelter and clap everyone else in.

Unfortunately some of our tenties didn't have as good a day as I'd enjoyed. One by one the brave warriors returned home, only to be temporarily inconvenienced by one or two having severe vasovagal episodes on finishing. *This is the collapse of the cardiovascular system after prolonged maintaining of blood pressure under stress and exercise. When the exercise ceases, the forced blood flow return to the heart abruptly stops, the fluid pools in the dilated vasculature of the lower extremities and the patient collapses in an undignified heap.* I did some basic helping as seemed appropriate (taking shoes and tight items of clothing off, dousing with water, offering of drinks, force feeding of gels and nuts. Elevation of legs and dragging bodily into the shade. Fending off the medics, that kind of thing). They recovered like true Spartan warriors. We all sat around a bit like air crash victims, but with a general air of smugness.

The general consensus around the tent was never again. Not just the MdS, but ultras and even any running of any description. I went along with the general groupthink but had a nagging feeling that I'd be back for another go.

Well all loitered and hung around for a finish ceremony which didn't materialize as Patrick Bauer's greeting of every single competitor continued into the dusk. These finishers were still going at sun down and beyond. The address system blared a lot of loud rock music of variable styles, about twenty five feet from our tent. No chance then of a quick restorative bout of shut eye. The next part of the entertainment was a photomontage of the race which was shown on a big screen. This was followed by a pop band from Canada, not quite to everyone's taste, but definitely there was no chance of achieving the sleep we were all rather in need of. We seemed caught in the limbo of being too tired to go out to play and it was too noisy to get any sleep - this produced, I'm sad to say, a little surliness and sense of humor failure from me for which I apologize. I regret this now.

Day seven (solidarity day)

For the last time (this year) we rolled out of bed. Awakened by the sun and the now daily cries of '*yell ah yell ah*' from the blue uniformed Berbers who looked like a sort of synchronized display team of caretakers. Luckily we were not at all stiff from our previous week's efforts, so we breezily joined the queued for some breakfast and then donned our new clean blue t-shirts for the cameras and the walking solidarity day. We had a predictably long award ceremony and a lot of good natured standing around in the warming morning sun. The t-shirts were unsurprisingly in an already disgusting state before we even left camp. No one had washed in a week and we had simply changed a top. They weren't clean for long. They were of course made from cotton, which my body certainly went to town on and soaked with fresh sweat, which then mingled with the under layers of grime. Nice.

We shuffled our way across five miles of dunes to the buses. I'd pretty much recovered and of course felt like running. This wasn't quite in the spirit but I enjoyed a light jog. Came third today. Pretty good result I reckon.

Having been through my share of dark moments on the MdS and really missing my wife, I vowed to spend more time at home and only run 5k races thereafter. This of course lasted about a month before I entered by next multi-day ultra. Oops.

About the author

Thank you for reading my book.
If you enjoyed this, I would very much appreciate you leaving feedback on the Amazon website.

About the author

He entered the Marathon des Sables because it sounded so very hard. He's also afraid of dying and regretting not having made the most of his life. This sentiment seems to be fairly common among MdS competitors.

He ran the race aged 41. He'd run a little at University (two marathons), before losing the plot and diverting his attentions to drinking and socializing. He ran the London marathon about four years ago and it hurt so much that something had to be done. Realizing his tubby middle had to go, he took up running more regularly. He has about forty marathons and ultramarathons under his belt so far.

By day, he's a General Practitioner in the South UK. In his spare time he reads more about running than is really healthy or good for him. His poor wife. He should probably get out more (*though obviously he thinks that means on the trails*).

If you have feedback, comments, questions or suggestions, please email phil@brainsolutions.co.uk

———————————————

Check out brainsolutions.co.uk for more titles by Dr Phil Harley

coming soon ...

BetterDay - stress management for busy people

Skinny Genes - real weight loss for real people in the real world (*out now*)

Do it, do it, DO IT! - A procrastinator's guide do world domination

Beginners guide to running (*out now*)

Stand Up, Sexy - better posture to cure back pain, improve prowess and agility

Centurion injuries - ultrarunning problems suffered by mortals

Phil Harley

14915756R00165

Printed in Great Britain
by Amazon.co.uk, Ltd.,
Marston Gate.